THE
POWER
OF THE
Lamb

D1547601

THE
POWER
OF THE *Lamb*

Edited by
John E. Toews
and
Gordon Nickel

Kindred Press

Winnipeg, MB, Canada   Hillsboro, KS, U.S.A.

THE POWER OF THE LAMB

Published simultaneously by Kindred Press, Winnipeg, Manitoba, R2L 2E5 and Kindred Press, Hillsboro, Kansas, 67063.

Cover Design: "Peaceable Kingdom" by Edward Hicks, copyright, New York State Historical Association, Cooperstown. Used by permission.

Printed in Canada by The Christian Press, Winnipeg.

International Standard Book Number: 0-919797-50-4

We've a song to be sung to the nations,
That shall lift their hearts to the Lord;
A song that shall conquer evil
And shatter the spear and sword,
And shatter the spear and sword.

CONTENTS

John E. Toews

Answering a Call for Teaching

The year was 1980. The place was Minneapolis. The occasion was a denominational conference of the Mennonite Brethren Churches of the US. The major issue was the peace position of the Mennonite Brethren Church.

The concern was the shape of the peace position in the post-Vietnam and post-draft era. The leaders of the Conference offered a resolution for the guidance of young men facing registration that strongly counseled the conscientious objector stance and alternative service as affirmed in the Confession of Faith.

Some lay people and some pastors thought it was time to relax the Mennonite Brethren commitment. After all, many of them had served in the military in World War II, and the men in uniform needed the gospel as much as any people. Furthermore, some worried that the peace confession of the Mennonite Brethren Church was a barrier to evangelism.

The long debate ended in an overwhelming resolution to affirm the Confession of Faith. The resolution included a request for clearer and more systematic teaching on the peace position.

This book is a response to the request for more teaching. The

Board of Church Ministries, the Conference in interim, commissioned this book in 1981 as one means of addressing the call for teaching materials.

A case study

The Mennonite Brethren Church is an historic peace church together with the other Mennonite churches, the Church of the Brethren and the Quakers. That means these churches have confessed on the basis of their understanding of the Bible that war is wrong. Therefore, these churches have refused participation in war and sought alternative ways of responding to war.

The internal debate regarding the peace position among Mennonite Brethren is not unique among the peace churches. As the peace churches have been acculturated into American society some have been tempted to weaken or even abandon the peace position. There are several causes for this temptation: a desire to be more American; a fear that the peace position is an obstacle to evangelism and church growth; and a confusion of the ethnic customs of many church members with distinctive theological understandings. Somehow the theological gets linked with the ethnic, and people desiring freedom from the ethnic think they also must reject the biblical teaching on peace.

The Mennonite Brethren are a case study of this struggle. Appendix II shows how consistently and frequently the Church's Confession of Faith and denominational statements have affirmed the peace position, and even strengthened the stance. Yet a 1982 church member survey showed that only 54 percent of the church believe participation in war is wrong, and only 43 percent agree that the church should actively promote peace.

Evangelicals embrace peace

The internal struggle with the peace position among peace churches, and the Mennonite Brethren Church specifically, is taking place during a time in history when the larger evangelical world is moving toward it in part and in whole. The renewal of social concern and spirituality in evangelicalism symbolized by *The Other Side, Sojourners,* and the Evangelicals for Social Action, reflects a deep commitment to biblical pacifism, and expresses profound indebtedness to the Anabaptist-Mennonite Church for this teaching.

Major mainstream evangelical leaders—Billy Graham, the late David Watson, John R.W. Stott, Michael Green, Vernon Grounds, to name only a few—have declared themselves nuclear pacifists and/or biblical pacifists. Two leading Canadian evangelicals in 1984 thanked the Mennonite Brethren Church for its contribution of the peace teaching and social concern to evangelicals of Canada. The past editor-in-chief of England's largest Christian publishing house recently expressed public gratitude for the biblical peace vision which the Mennonites are giving to the world.

Purpose of this book

The purpose of this book is to make the case for the biblical peace position for Mennonite Brethren who are struggling with its importance or even validity, and for evangelical Christians who are embracing it as a biblical teaching. It is presented from a particular context—the Mennonite Brethren Church—in the hope that it will strengthen and nurture the Mennonite Brethren and the evangelical churches' commitment and faithfulness to follow Jesus in loving the enemy whoever he or she may be.

The conviction behind this purpose is anchored in the belief that Jesus' peace teaching is central to the gospel and to the mission of the church. "The gospel of peace"—restored relationships with God, humanity and nature—is the good news of God's gift in Jesus Christ. That gospel cannot be fractured by announcing salvation without wholeness, without peace for all people in all relationships.

One of the deepest crises of our time is the crisis of violence. The mission of the church is to announce the good news that in Jesus there is another way. It is the way of peace in all relationships—personal, social, national and international.

The Bible is the norm

The structure of the book reflects the context from which it comes and the people it seeks to address. Five chapters are devoted to biblical teaching because for Mennonite Brethren and evangelicals the Bible is the sole and ultimate authority for questions of belief and practice. Jesus is the starting point for reading and interpreting the Bible. He is the clearest and ultimate revelation of the will of God for his people and for humanity. Jesus taught and lived the way of peace, and called the disciple community he established to live by his word and example. Jesus' word and model is normative for the church.

The teachings of the Old Testament, often read as justifying war, foreshadow, and in fact, teach the way of peace for God's people, as shown in the chapters by Elmer Martens. This interpretation of the Old Testament represents a very important contribution to the proper interpretation of the Bible. Jesus, the patriarchs and the prophets can no longer be pitted against each other, as in so much Protestant interpretation of the Bible.

A final chapter on the Bible shows that the New Testament church faithfully followed the teaching and example of Jesus. It consistently taught and practiced peace in all relationships inside and outside the church, and non-resistance to government and enemies.

The Bible speaks with one voice to questions of war and peace. From its center, Jesus, to its beginning and end, it proclaims that God's will is peace, not war.

Church history points to peace

Four chapters study the history of the church. The point they make is that the early church until the Emperor Constantine was a peace church, and that the Anabaptist-Mennonite-Mennonite Brethren churches have been peace churches since the Reformation. All Anabaptist-Mennonite-Mennonite Brethren confessions of faith have confessed the biblical teaching on peace as normative for Christians.

While church history is not a norm for faith and practice, as the

Bible is, the history of the church is important for two reasons. First, Anabaptist-Mennonites and many evangelicals believe "the fall of the church" occurred with Constantine. He married church and state. Citizenship in the state and membership in the church became synonymous. All people in the society became Christians and church members, not just those adults baptized on confession of faith in Jesus Christ as Savior and Lord. From Constantine to the present the church has been compromised by this marriage of church and state.

Secondly, Anabaptist-Mennonites and evangelicals believe that after the compromise of Constantine the faithful church finds its most authentic expression in the minority church. The true church is the believers' church that runs counter to the "Christianized-culture-church," the believers' church that insists that church membership is based on adult conversion and baptism into the church, and the believers' church that insists that church and state must be separate. Anabaptist-Mennonite-Mennonite Brethren church history is one small but important stream of the larger minority or counter-culture history of the church. The Anabaptist-Mennonite-Mennonite Brethren history bears witness to a consistent teaching and practice of biblical peacemaking. And it bears witness to the enormous cost in life of a faithfulness that runs counter to the mainstream church.

The just war theory does not work

From the Bible and church history the book moves to the important question of the "just war theory" which the mainstream history of the church has used to justify its support of and involvement in war. Howard Loewen convincingly makes the case that the just war theory does not offer the church effective guidance on questions of war in a nuclear and revolutionary age. Not only has the theory not worked to limit or prevent war in practice, but it falls far short of the biblical vision of peace.

The power of the lamb

The book concludes with a description of two alternative ways to live, by tiger power or lamb power, force or love, war or peace. In the book of Revelation Jesus appears not as a lion but as a lamb. Every Christian is called to follow the lamb in the way of sacrificial love.

There is a war going on in the universe, the writers of the New Testament tell us, but it is the war of the lamb. The war must be fought on his terms. We are not fighting a worldly war, Paul writes in 2 Corinthians 10, nor are our weapons knives, guns or bombs. The weapons Paul actually lists in Ephesians 6 are ridiculous by the standards of the world, yet Paul insists they have divine power to destroy enemy strongholds.

And the goal of the war we fight is not to kill men and women, nor even to protect our lives and property. Rather, it is to take every thought captive to obey Jesus Christ as Lord.

LOVE YOUR ENEMY INTO THE KINGDOM

John E. Toews

The Teaching of Jesus on Peace

They'd seen him every day, teaching his words of life in the light of the temple courts. But when the chief priests finally came to arrest Jesus they came at night—along with a big crowd carrying swords and clubs. Jesus' disciples had a good idea of what was up, and they were scared out of their wits. Peter drew his sword and swung it at the servant of the high priest, cutting off his ear. "Stop that!" Jesus rebuked Peter. "Put your sword back into its sheath: for all who draw the sword shall die by the sword. Don't you know that if I wanted to, I could ask my Father for a hundred thousand angels to fight for me?" Instead, Jesus healed the servant's ear, and let the mob take him.

Jesus is the center of the Christian faith. Everything before him points to him, and everything after him flows from him. Jesus is the measuring stick for Christian thinking and action. Therefore, Christian peace teaching and witness must be anchored in Jesus.

"Peace" is an important word for Jesus. It is used 91 times in the New Testament—more often than most other words related to salvation. "Life" is used 135 times in the New Testament, "righteousness" 91, "gospel" 76, "salvation" 45, "cross" 27, "reconciliation" 4, "propitiation" or "expiation" 4 and "ransom" 4 times.

Jesus means peace. To follow Jesus means to be a peacemaker.

Because Jesus is the standard, we need to begin the study of the Bible's teaching on peace with some of his words. Read them carefully.

The Kingdom of God

"The time is fulfilled, and the Kingdom of God is at hand; repent, and believe in the gospel" (Mark 1:15).

The central message of Jesus is that the Kingdom of God is present. The Kingdom of God as Jesus spoke of it refers to a reign, not a territory. The reign of God entered the world in a new way with Jesus. The way of the Kingdom is explained in the teachings of Jesus.

Jesus is a Warrior

"I saw Satan fall like lightening from heaven" (Luke 10:18).

"And he came to Nazareth, where he had been brought up, and he went into the synagogue, as his custom was, on the sabbath day. And he stood up to read; and there was given to him the book of the prophet Isaiah. He opened the book, and found the place where it is written, 'The Spirit of the Lord is upon me, because he has anointed me to preach good news to the poor. He has sent me to proclaim release to the captives and recovery of sight to the blind, to set at liberty those who are oppressed, to proclaim the acceptable year of the Lord" (Luke 4:16-19).

God is pictured as a warrior in the Old Testament. He fights against the enemies of his people and wins the victory for them.

Jesus is presented as a warrior in the Gospels. He does battle against Satan and demonic powers, and he defeats them. Jesus' miracles of healing and casting out demons represent victories over Satan and his powers (Mark 1:23-28; Luke 10:18). These victories are promises of the final victory that will occur at the second coming of Christ when he comes on the clouds of heaven (Mark 13; Matthew 24; Luke 21). In the Old Testament God appeared on the clouds of heaven as a warrior, and that image is now applied to Jesus.

The war that Jesus fights is a war with Satan and the powers of

Satan's kingdom. Jesus' victorious war with demonic forces means peace has been won. Jesus teaches his followers to live in peace and to be peacemakers.

The Peacemaker

"Blessed are the peacemakers for they shall be called sons of God" (Matthew 5:9).

Jesus starts his teaching about peace with this seventh beatitude in the Sermon on the Mount. The beatitudes of Matthew 5 show the kind of life that a disciple of Jesus is to live.

The blessing at the beginning of each beatitude describes an attitude of well-being or salvation given by God. The blessing is followed by virtues (meek, merciful, peacemaker, etc.) which indicate the recommended lifestyle for the disciple.

Following the blessing and virtue is a description of the salvation that God will give. We could translate this beatitude something like this: "present salvation to the ones making peace because they will be called sons of God."

"Peacemaker" is a rare word. The word "peace" means well-being, wholeness or completeness, and is often linked with words like "righteousness" and "salvation." "Make" is the word for all activity in the Bible. "Peacemaking" is never neutral. It describes either "doing" the will of God or rejecting it.

Who is a peacemaker? He or she does not simply live in peace or practice nonresistance, but actually makes peace. To be a peacemaker means to establish peace between unfriendly people. The phrase does not describe people who promote human happiness, nor even people who help others to find peace with God, important as that is. Rather, it means to come between angry and fighting people in order to make peace.

Why be a peacemaker?

The reward promised to a peacemaker is that he or she will be called a "son or daughter of God." The title "son of God" is given only by God himself. God uses it to mean a special family-type relationship of loving and free communication between himself and his children. The Bible uses this term very carefully, usually to mean a gift granted only at the Last Judgment.

The peacemaker shall be called a son of God. He or she will have a special relationship with God at the Last Judgment. Only in the "love your enemy" text does this miracle take place in the present as a reward for obedience.

If our beatitude is translated literally it reads something like this: "present salvation to the ones actively making peace among fighting people because they will be called the sons of God in the final judgment." People who enjoy God's salvation are called to be peacemakers now because in the end they will be granted a special relationship with God.

Our beatitude is near the center of the introduction to the Sermon on the Mount. The introduction concludes with 5:16, "let your light so shine before men that they may see your good works and give glory to your father who is in heaven."

Many people have suggested that verse 16 is the theme of the sermon. What follows is a picture of how disciples are to behave if they want to be the light of the world. Three other passages in Matthew help us see what peacemaking is all about: 1) rejecting retaliation (5:38-43); 2) loving the enemy (5:43-48); and 3) proclaiming the Kingdom and peace as a missionary (10:1-15).

Do not resist

> "You have heard that it was said, 'an eye for an eye and a tooth for a tooth.' But I say to you, Do not resist one who is evil. But if anyone strikes you on the right cheek, turn to him the other also; and if anyone would sue you and take your coat, let him have your cloak as well; and if anyone forces you to go one mile, go with him two miles" (Matthew 5:38-41).

The way to make peace is first explained by Jesus' command, "do not resist an evil person" (5:38). Jesus says that a peacemaker must give up all resistance against bad treatment.

Jesus sets aside the law of retaliation, which allowed a person to pay back an injury in kind. That law was given Israel by God to limit revenge to a just and clearly defined punishment. But now Jesus says "don't pay back the evil-doer." Rather, accept wrong-doing as Jesus did.

Jesus then gives four examples of nonresistance to wrong-doing:

* Example one says, don't resist the insult of a backhanded slap in the face. Turn the other cheek instead.

* Example two teaches surrender of everything rather than insistence on legal rights. The coat was both an article of clothing and a covering at night. It could not be taken according to Jewish law. But Jesus says, give it up rather than sue.

* Example three urges acceptance of a draft into temporary military service. Jesus rejects the practice of many Jews who not only refused such service, but encouraged violence against the soldiers demanding assistance. Jesus says, do not resist, but go two miles instead.

* Example four says, give money instead of lending it when a loan is requested.

More difficult instructions could hardly have been given by Jesus in first century Palestine. The Jews were oppressed by the Romans. Their oppression was comparable to the kind of oppression that many people experience in communist or third-world dictatorships today.

Jesus says, do not strike back when you are brutally oppressed; do not oppose the violation of basic personal and legal rights. Luke adds a further word to those recorded in Matthew: do this because God is a God of mercy (Luke 6.32-38). Since that is who God is, be like him. Refuse to take revenge.

Love the enemy

"You have heard that it was said, 'You shall love your neighbor and hate your enemy.' But I say to you, Love your enemies and pray for those who persecute you, so that you may be sons of your Father who is in heaven" (Matthew 5:43-44).

If refusing to retaliate sounds like a hard command, the next is even harder. Jesus says making peace means loving the enemy.

What Jesus has in mind here has to do with more than personal relations. The focus is not on the person who does the loving—on the victory over self. Nor does "love the enemy" mean simply nonresistance in the face of hostility and brutality. Jesus is not speaking only about what Christians should do when they experience opposition.

Jesus also is speaking about life in society at large. He rejects a teaching in the Judaism of his day which encouraged hatred of and violence against the enemy.

Two groups of people in Jesus' world, called Essenes (the people of the Dead Sea Scrolls community) and Zealots, taught Jews to hate and murder the enemy. The ultimate enemy, of course, was the Roman soldier or government agent, or anyone who assisted him, such as a tax collector.

The command to love the enemy is a command not to get sucked into nationalistic hatred of the enemy. Jesus is publicly breaking with the leaders in his world who teach and practice hatred of and violence against the enemy.

But Jesus is asking for more than nonresistance in the face of violence. He commands active love of the enemy. In Matthew that love of the enemy is defined as praying for him or her. Luke adds "do good, bless, lend money, and expect nothing in return." It means to not accept the enemy as he or she is. Love seeks to transform the hatred of the enemy.

Friendship evangelism

To love the enemy means to be a missionary to the enemy and love him or her into the Kingdom of God. Jesus commands friendship evangelism for the enemy. He says, do not just love the neighbor; everyone does that. Love, befriend and evangelize the enemy.

Peacemakers evangelize because they are given sonship by God. Jesus says peacemakers become sons of God with him now, not just in the Last Judgment. The act of loving the enemy is such a good demonstration of peacemaking that the end-time gift of sonship is granted immediately.

Peacemakers become what Jesus is because they do what he does—they love the enemy and suffer with and for him in order to transform him. That's exactly what Jesus did for us when we were enemies of God. Jesus calls his disciples to do the same.

Luke adds an interesting explanation by Jesus. Jesus repeatedly asks, "what credit is that to you?" He assumes that there should be something special about the lives of disciples. If disciples are good only the way everybody else is good, what credit is that?

"Credit" here does not mean the ability to earn God's salvation, but behavior that communicates the mercy of God. What kind of behavior communicates the gospel? What is it about the disciple lifestyle that reflects the nature of God? Jesus answer is, *loving the enemy.* It is special behavior that reflects the nature of God and thus communicates the gospel.

Preach the gospel

The evangelistic nature of peacemaking becomes clearer in Matthew 10, where Jesus sends his disciples out to evangelize. They are to travel light, which means giving total energy to being a missionary and being dependent on other people. The message of the missionary is the Kingdom of God and peace. Overcome Satan, the real and the big enemy, by preaching this message, says Jesus.

Finally, the missionary is to be careful about his or her audience. Bless with peace those who hear. Receive peace back from those who do not hear, and leave them. Give them an end-time curse, which means taking the peace blessing back, and abandon them to their hostility.

Jesus never fooled his disciples about the popularity of this missionary strategy and message. It will result in persecution for the missionary, he warned, and it will divide the people who hear it.

In Matthew's Gospel Jesus calls his disciples to be peacemakers. A peacemaker is a Christian who makes peace between fighting people, who rejects revenge and retaliation, who loves the enemy, who proclaims peace in his or her missionary activity and message.

Peace is central in Jesus' definition of discipleship. It characterizes the disciple's lifestyle and mission. It shapes the way he relates to friend and enemy and how he proclaims the gospel.

On earth peace

Let's have a look at Luke's Gospel. "Peace" is used 14 times in Luke in contrast to the four in Matthew. The first uses in Luke come with the announcement of the Jesus' birth.

In 1:79 "peace" is the last word of the human announcement of Jesus' coming birth. It is linked to rescue from enemies, to righteousness, to salvation, to forgiveness of sins, and to light for those in darkness. Jesus will fulfill the messianic prophecies of the Old Testament about a reign of peace.

If "peace" summarizes the human announcement of Jesus' birth, it is the key word in the divine commentary on his birth in 2:14. Jesus brings peace, not only to Israel, as Zechariah prophesied, but to all people on earth. Simeon, prophesying by divine inspiration in 2:29ff., asks to die in peace because Israel's messianic hopes have been fulfilled.

Peace here is associated with revelation to the Gentiles and glory to Israel; it means the fulfillment of Israel's hopes and salvation for the Gentiles. Luke introduces his gospel by proclaiming Jesus as the peacemaker for all peoples.

Go in peace

After Luke introduces Jesus as the peacemaker he illustrates in three passages how Jesus lived and taught peace.

In chapters 7 and 8 Jesus brings peace to sinful and ill people. Twice Jesus says, "go in peace." The first statement is made to a prostitute who washes his feet (7:50). The second word is to a woman with a continual menstrual flow (8:48). In the first instance peace comes as forgiveness of sins and salvation, while in the second it comes as physical healing. Peace means wholeness in two different ways for two different people.

Peace to this house

The second group of peace texts appears in a special "journey to Jerusalem" report that is unique to Luke's Gospel (9:51-19:44). The fact that this trip is reported only in Luke means it is important in Luke's portrait of Jesus. It is significant, therefore, that this trip is introduced and concluded with peace words from Jesus.

At the start of the trip Jesus appoints 70 disciples to proclaim the gospel. The gospel message is peace (10:5-6). The mission to the nations (70 symbolizes a world-wide mission) has peace as its distinguishing feature.

The special travel report concludes with two peace declarations. The first ends the triumphal entry chorus of Jesus' disciples. Jesus as King means "peace in heaven" (19:38). Remember, "peace on earth" announced Jesus' arrival in 2:14.

The second peace declaration is that Jesus comes to Jerusalem to establish peace. But Jerusalem does not accept his peace (19:42). Therefore, Jesus weeps over Jerusalem, and proceeds to cleanse the temple.

Within the Jerusalem travel report Luke records two other peace words of Jesus. In 11:21 we are told that Satan's (Beelzebub's) house is not a house of peace because God's Kingdom that is coming now in Jesus is stronger than Satan. Peace here denotes security and safety from the power of Satan.

Peace is an alternative to war in 14:32. It shows up in a story about the necessity of counting the cost of following Jesus.

Peace be with you

The final peace passage in Luke comes after the resurrection of Jesus. Christ appears among his disciples just before his ascension, and says, "peace be with you" (24:36). The Bearer of peace (2:14) who proclaims peace (10:5-6) but is rejected as the King of peace (19:38-42) is the Lord of peace. Therefore, his farewell speech is "peace."

"Peace" is central to the mission and ministry of Jesus in Luke. It is linked to liberation from oppression, fulfillment of Israel's messianic hopes, salvation for the gentiles, forgiveness of sins, missionary witness, proper response to Jesus, and the presence of the risen Christ among his followers.

Jesus means peace—peace as wholeness in all relationships and dimensions of life.

John E. Toews

The Meaning of Jesus' Peace Teaching

"Jesus stood before the Roman governor who questioned him, 'Are you the king of the Jews?' he asked. 'So you say,' answered Jesus. But he said nothing in response to the accusations of the chief priests and elders. So Pilate said to him, 'Don't you hear all these things they accuse you of?' But Jesus refused to answer a single word, with the result that the Governor was greatly surprised....They crucified him....Jesus gave a loud cry and breathed his last. Then the curtain hanging in the Temple was torn in two from top to bottom. The earth shook....When the army officer and the soldiers with him who were watching Jesus saw the earthquake and everything else that happened, they were terrified and said, 'He really was the Son of God!'"

We have studied briefly the teachings of Jesus about peace in the Gospels of Matthew and Luke. The big question is, what do these words of Jesus mean? What did they mean in Jesus' day? What do they mean today?

Let's take the second question first—what do they mean today? The peace words of Jesus are now understood in one of four main ways.

1) *The spiritualist interpretation.* This view states that Jesus called people to inner peace through personal conversion. Spiritual renewal implies peace with one's fellow human beings. Peace with the neighbor is understood in terms of personal, one-to-one relationships.

2) *The social gospel interpretation.* Jesus called people to change society, says this view. The world must be changed from a place of oppression and evil to one of peace, justice and love. This change must come about by human effort that is motivated by the love of God revealed in Jesus. The cleansing of society will make personal conversion possible. The elimination of evil in society will make possible peace in personal, social and spiritual relationships.

3) *The revolutionary interpretation.* Jesus called people to revolt and violently overthrow the oppressive Roman government, according to this view. Jesus was a revolutionary Zealot—a first-century guerrilla fighter. The gospels conceal the truly violent revolutionary Jesus in order to make Christianity acceptable in the Roman Empire, this view claims. What Jesus really calls people to is revolutionary violence in order to overthrow all forms of oppression so that God may bring in his Kingdom of peace, justice and love.

4) *The Kingdom community interpretation.* This view says that Jesus asked people to respond to the presence of God's Kingdom by repenting, by believing and by entering the disciple community. Peacemaking was the lifestyle of this disciple community in all relationships.

The Kingdom way

Which of these four ways is most faithful to the Jesus of the Gospels?

The words of Jesus on peace are best explained by the fourth interpretation. The Kingdom of God that Jesus brought involved the creation of a new order of living together in the world. At the center of this new way of life is Jesus' teaching to love God and neighbor.

The radical intent of Jesus' teaching is seen most clearly in the command to love the enemy. The enemy is not just the neighbor who makes me angry. The neighbor is the foreigner who threatens my life and the lives of the people around me.

At the center of the Jesus way is not the heroic style of living alone by love in the face of evil and violence. Rather, it is the creation of a new order of living together in the world. It involves the formation of a disciple community in the world which calls other people to enter the Kingdom commuity.

This new community of God's people is to live out here on earth the teachings and example of Jesus. It does so in anticipation of the present and coming Kingdom of God.

The new order of life, or the new disciple community, created by Jesus had all the marks of a new movement intent on changing the world. It challenged the basic assumptions of the existing society; it challenged even the continued existence of the family, the most stable social unit in Jewish society (remember how Jesus told his disciples to choose him over father and mother, brother and sister?).

The challenge of the Jesus way was so sharp that Jesus was crucified as a political criminal; crucifixion was reserved for the crime of treason.

The way of the cross

Jesus accepted his death lovingly and nonviolently. In fact, the Gospels report that Jesus gave his life—it was not taken from him. He absorbed humanity's hatred into his death and so set men and women free. Jesus gave people the freedom to do the ultimate—to kill him. He took the fear and hatred of humanity into his own body and thereby stopped it.

Jesus took this stance instead of calling in the armies of God because his plan of action was determined by the Suffering Servant of Isaiah 53. He saw his own death as a death for others, a death that would redeem humanity from sin and violence and for God and peace.

The death of Jesus on the cross represents the defenselessness and nonviolence of God. On the cross Jesus shows us what God is like, and in the process gives people an option: they are no longer compelled to kill. They can respond to hatred and violence lovingly and nonviolently in the power of God just as Jesus did.

Jesus is the proclaimer and the teacher of a new way in the world. But he is more than that. Jesus is the new way in the world.

Jesus in the first century

The Jesus way includes personal salvation and a right spiritual relationship with God. But that's not all. The Jesus way is a new way of being and living together as the people of God in the world.

That is the most obvious meaning of the words Jesus used. His language refers to a very real option for society. Jesus talks about a kingdom, about loyalty, about serving, about lording, about just and loving relationships, about discerning where God's people are in the world, about sharing one's resources, about loving and praying for one's enemies.

The Jesus way is described in language that suggests a new way for God's people to be in the world. They live in the world as peacemakers in all relationships and in all situations.

The shape of Jesus' world

The newness of the Jesus way may be seen most clearly in contrast to the prevailing violence of his time.

Jesus' world was a violent one.

Palestine was occupied by the Romans from 63 B.C. The occupation contradicted Jewish faith. The law of Moses was the revealed constitution of Israel. According to the law, the Jewish people were to be ruled by God through his anointed leader. No foreigner was to rule over the Jews.

The occupation introduced social tensions. Jewish ethnic and religious identity was threatened by the presence of Gentiles and by pagan practices. The result was open antagonism between Jews and Gentiles.

The occupation created an unbearable tax burden. Jewish law required heavy tithes and taxes: the "first fruits" offering (one to three percent of a crop); a 10 percent tithe of all produce or earnings every year; and a second tithe of 10 percent every year, the annual Temple tax. The amount of tax required by Jewish law was over 20 percent.

To this system of taxation the Romans added an additional 25 percent, including crop and land taxes, and poll taxes. In addition, the Roman army, which involved thousands of civilians as well— wives, concubines, children, servants, slaves, merchants, doctors, veterinarians, etc.—could demand food, and could press animals and people into service. The Jews of Jesus' day were subject to two systems of taxation. The burden was extraordinary. All told, Jews were expected to pay a minimum of 45-50 percent tax a year.

Many Jews could survive only by tax protest. The taxes they did not pay were the Jewish ones, since they could protest the Roman taxes only at the risk of death. Jews became disloyal to the law to survive. The price for this disobedience was exclusion from synagogue and Temple. Such excluded people became known as "the people of the land," and were viewed as unclean by the Jewish authorities. The double taxation system, in addition to causing great economic hardship, thus also served to divide and fragment Jewish society.

The growing violence

The Roman occupation of Palestine led to violent resistance. This resistance was not confined to a small revolutionary party, but embraced people from all segments and all parties of the population. The resistance was especially intense from the accession of Herod the Great in 37 B.C. to the outbreak of the Jewish-Roman War in 66 A.D.

The reign of Herod the Great was one of terror (recall, for example, the slaughter of the children in Bethlehem following the birth of Jesus in Matthew 2:16-18). Revolts erupted throughout the country at Herod's death in 4 B.C. The Romans punished the revolt by killing 3000 Jews in the Temple and by crucifying 2000 Jews outside Jerusalem. The introduction of direct Roman taxation in 6 A.D. (the census of Luke 2) was greeted by a revolt led by Judas the Galilean and a Pharisee named Saddok. Massive non-violent protests were directed against the policies of various Roman governors, especially Pilate and Caligula.

A guerrilla movement, known as the Zealots, emerged at the time of the census for taxation in 6 A.D. The Zealots waged guerrilla warfare, and sometimes pitched battles, against the Romans and their Jewish supporters. Many of these zealots believed in "holy war." They took as their models the high priest Phinehas, who killed an Israelite and pagan woman for living together and led Israel in a holy war against the Midianites (Numbers 25 and 31), and Elijah, who killed the prophets of Baal (I Kings 18).

The Zealots taught that Roman occupation violated the first commandment (have no other gods), that Roman taxation violated the second commandment (have no graven images) because Roman money had images on it, that circumcision whether voluntary or involuntary was necesssary to prevent the desecration of the land and the law, that pious Jews must be totally separated from heathen, and that God would cooperate with the Jews in freeing Palestine from Roman rule if they would initiate armed revolt (which they did in 66 A.D.).

The revolutionary fervor stirred by such zealot thinking was intensified by revolutionary prophets who claimed to be the messiah. Seven such "messianic pretenders" are known from the period prior to the 66-70 Jewish-Roman war. All promised to lead the Jewish people to military victory over the Romans.

The religious zealots who fanned the revolutionary spirit of first century Judaism were not confined to the Zealot party, as many have suggested. Rather they represent a wide cross-section of Jewish people and parties. Pharisees, Sadducees and Essenes, as well as Zealots are identified as part of this spreading and growing violence and revolt.

The quest for holiness

The resistance to Rome was widespread because it was built on a deep and profound spiritual quest in Judaism. Jewish people in Jesus' time, as in earlier times, were concerned to order their corporate and individual lives so as to be loyal to God, so as to imitate God. The content of this imitation was defined as holiness. Holiness in turn was defined as separation from everything impure. The quest for holiness as separation from uncleanness was the theological and cultural dynamic of Jewish life in Jesus' time. It also was the engine which drove the growing resistance against Rome.

The quest for holiness was based on Leviticus 19:2, "be holy because, I, the Lord your God, am holy." God was holy. God's people must be holy. For God's people to be holy, the law, the Temple and the land must be holy. And the holiness of law, Temple and land depended on the careful observance of the law by the people. All major parties in first century Judaism were committed to this theology.

The two major renewal movements of Jesus' time, the Pharisees and the Essenes, were both committed to an intensification of holiness as part of their quest. All Israel was to live as priests. That is, all people were to live by the laws governing the priesthood rather than the laity.

The intensification of the quest for holiness had two major consequences in Judaism. First, it produced marked internal divisions between the holy and unholy in Jewish society, e.g., Pharisees and Essenes compared to "the people of the land," sinners and tax collectors. Secondly, it pushed Judaism increasingly toward a collision with Rome because Roman occupation compromised the quest for holiness.

The Jesus alternative

Now we can answer the first question we asked at the beginning of this chapter—what did Jesus' peace words mean in his day? Jesus offered God's people, the Jews, an alternative to the quest for holiness by replacing holiness with mercy. Instead of "you shall be holy because I am holy" Jesus said, "be merciful, just as your father is merciful" (Luke 6:36). He also redefined holiness as power to overcome uncleanness rather than as separation from uncleanness. Therefore, he moved freely among the unclean to release the power of God to forgive and triumph over uncleanness.

Jesus' substitution of mercy for holiness as central to imitating

God had two major consequences that reversed the consequences of the Jewish quest for holiness. First, mercy was inclusive, not exclusive. It was forgiving and accepting. Therefore, Jesus welcomed and called all people, clean and unclean, Jew and Gentile, into his kingdom community. Secondly, mercy meant the rejection of violence. Jesus taught "love of enemy;" he rejected the violence of Israel and his disciples; he died as a demonstration of the loving mercy and non-violence of God.

The Jesus way meant a new alternative which his life and death demonstrated for the world. The new alternative introduced was the life of peacemaking, the life of suffering love, based on the loving mercy of God.

Jesus' peace teaching today

The call to follow Jesus is the call to the Jesus way of peacemaking and suffering love together with God's people, the church. When we confess that Jesus is Lord we voluntarily reject coercion and violence as ways of living in the world, and accept that way which has Jesus as its center and the cross as its high point.

That means that biblical peacemaking is centered first and foremost in Jesus as Messiah and Lord. Of course, not all peace movements and causes, however noble, are Jesus-centered or Christian movements. The kind of peacemaking that the Bible talks about can be known only in relation to Jesus as Lord.

Where Jesus is Lord, peacemaking is the only way of life within the Kingdom community and in the relation of the Kingdom community to the world.

GOD'S GOAL IS SHALOM

Elmer A. Martens

Voices for Peace in the Old Testament

The King of Syria was getting frustrated. He was trying to fight Israel, but every time he came up with a good battle plan, a prophet in Israel by the name of Elisha would miraculously reveal it to the Israelite army. The Syrian king with his army set out to capture Elisha at Dothan. But as the Syrians approached the city, God struck them blind in answer to Elisha's prayer. When the king of Israel saw that the enemy soldiers were now sitting ducks, he asked Elisha, "Shall I kill them?" The prophet said, "Forget it, king. Do not kill them. Give them something to eat and drink, then send them back to their master" (2 Kings 6:22). The advice of Elisha didn't amount to much in terms of military strategy, but it worked anyway. It produced peace. The Bible reports, "So the bands from Aram stopped raiding Israel's territory."

It is quite easy to see that Jesus wanted his followers to be a people of peace. But what about the Old Testament? What does it have to say about the question of peace and war?

Bible-believing Christians must face the Old Testament squarely. When Paul wrote that all Scripture is inspired by God, he had the Old Testament in mind. Paul wrote that the Old Testament teaches, rebukes, corrects and trains people in righteousness (2 Timothy 3:16). Jesus certainly never put down the Old Testament.

War and peace

Many wars are reported in the Old Testament. Under Moses' command, Israel fought the Amalekites. Under Joshua's command, the Israelite army defeated the Canaanites. The prophet Samuel hacked Agag, a king, to pieces (1 Samuel 15:33). Who hasn't heard the stories of David and Goliath and the victory of Israel over the Philistines?

Are these reports meant to be instructions for us? In the Old Testament God commanded his people to fight. Doesn't that mean that he could also command Christians to fight today?

Under what circumstances did God command people to fight? Did he always command war? Were there any times when he gave instructions about peace?

There are voices for war in the Old Testament, but there are also voices for peace. Could it be that we have listened so closely to the war voices that we have missed the voices for peace? Before we tackle the hard question of wars in the Old Testament in the next chapter, let's gather information about God's will for peace.

Some of the voices for peace were prophets, and others were the wisdom teachers. The historical books of the Old Testament tell stories of people who followed the way of peace. One way or another, at various points in Israel's history God said a strong "no" to war.

Advice to follow peaceful ways

About 600 years before the time of Jesus a prophet named Jeremiah was asked for advice. The Babylonians had invaded Israel. The enemy had destroyed Jerusalem, burned the temple, and taken Israel's ruling class captive to Babylon 700 miles away. Jeremiah, however, stayed in Jerusalem.

Jeremiah wrote a letter to these exiles on how to conduct themselves in the foreign land. The exiles were nervous: apparently some of them even wanted to revolt against Babylon. Jeremiah's advice must have come as a surprise. He advised the exiles to settle down, build homes, plant gardens and "seek the peace and prosperity of the city to which I have carried you into exile. Pray to the Lord for it, because if it prospers you too will prosper" (Jeremiah 29:7).

Jeremiah counseled the exiled Israelites to pray for the enemy—but how could they pray for Babylon if they hated it? Surely such counsel is a hint of what Jesus would say later: "Love your enemies."

Zechariah, a prophet who lived in Jerusalem after the return of the exiles, also counseled peaceful ways. His words, spoken in the name of God, asked the people to "speak the truth to each other and render true and sound judgment in your courts" (Zechariah 8:16). Zechariah then gave the crisp instruction, "Therefore love truth and peace" (8:19).

The book of Proverbs, likely written long before Jeremiah, gives advice on peaceful living. One example is Proverbs 25:21: "If your enemy is hungry, give him food to eat; if he is thirsty, give him water to drink"—an instruction that goes against a person's normal impulses.

Examples of helping the enemy

One incident in which this kind of advice was applied during an international war occured in the story of Elisha, quoted at the beginning of this chapter. Another application came during a civil war between Israel and Judah.

Israel had won the war, but when the victorious officers returned to Samaria, their capital city, the prophet Oded had a message for them. Oded admitted that Israel was God's agent in punishing Judah, then added, "But you have slaughtered them in a rage that reaches to heaven" (2 Chronicles 28:9). Oded advised them to return the prisoners of war, "for the Lord's anger rests on you" (2 Chronicles 28:11).

In response, the leaders "took the prisoners, and from the plunder they clothed all who were naked. They provided them with clothes and sandles, food and drink and healing balm" and led them in peace to Jericho, a city in Judah. Didn't this match the teaching from Proverbs, "if your enemy is hungry, give him food to eat"?

These two stories illustrate the advice of Psalm 34:14: "turn from evil and do good; seek peace and pursue it."

Prophets saw peaceful days ahead

While wisdom teachers counseled peace, God's prophets envisioned an age of peace. Isaiah, for example, painted an attractive picture of a peaceful era which differs sharply from the usual ideas of how to get to the ideal society.

It is from Isaiah's pen that the well-known verse comes:

They will beat their swords into plowshares
And their spears into pruning hooks.
Nation will not take up sword against nation,
Nor will they train for war any more (Isaiah 2:4).

Isaiah's vision of peace is special because it pictures people streaming to the temple to learn about God's ways. Isaiah describes how "the mountain of the house of the Lord"—Jerusalem where the temple stands—will be raised higher than the hills.

By this Isaiah doesn't mean that Jerusalem will rise into the sky, but that it will be a major center of interest and that out from it will go God's word. Nations from all over will come to learn about God. What they learn will cause them to change their weapons of war into tools of agriculture.

This drastic change will come about because the world's people will turn to God. His will will now dominate and there will be no war. Obedience to God's teaching will bring about a warless society.

Many Christians feel that such a time of peace is predicted for the future millennium. And it's true that when God reigns in the millennium, war will be no more. But Isaiah's vision is not only for the end times. Isaiah explains that *whenever* and *wherever* people will seek God and his ways, they will, in obedience to God, lay down weapons and not learn war anymore.

The prince who suffers

There is a further difference between Isaiah's picture of the peaceful age and that given by philosophers and dreamers. Isaiah's peaceful age is linked with a person.

In his vision Isaiah sees the wolf lie down with the lamb and the cow and the bear graze together (Isaiah 11:6-9). A baby grabs a snake to play with and doesn't get bitten. In the animal world, just as in the world of people, "they will neither harm nor destroy on all my holy mountain." Beautiful!

But that peaceful scene is preceded by a description of the "branch of Jesse," a reference to the Messiah, who is described as one upon whom rests "the Spirit of wisdom and understanding, the Spirit of counsel and of power, the Spirit of knowledge and of the fear of the Lord" (Isaiah 11:2). He will judge people fairly. Indeed, "righteousness will be his belt and faithfulness the sash around his waist" (Isaiah 11:5).

It is the Prince of Peace who will make the peaceful age possible. At Christmas especially, we hear of the promise of a child to be born whose name is Wonderful Counselor...and Prince of Peace (Isaiah 9:6). Isaiah describes the Coming One as a royal figure but says—and this seems like a contradiction—he is also a suffering servant.

Easter reminds us that the Prince of Peace bore our griefs and sorrows. God loaded our sins on him, and he carried them, says Isaiah, "like a lamb led to slaughter" (Isaiah 53:7). This servant was mistreated, but he did not fight back. The aim of his suffering was peace: "The punishment that brought us peace (*shalom*) was upon him" (Isaiah 53:5).

A great new word—"shalom"

Isaiah uses a word for peace that is very rich in meaning—*shalom*. This word is used in Isaiah 26 times; it is found elsewhere in the Old Testament a total of 240 times.

To translate it as "peace" is correct but not enough. *Shalom* has to do with a state of wholeness and well-being. *Shalom* speaks of harmony, health and a satisfying life. It means much more than the absence of war, though it includes that too. *Shalom means that all is well between a person and God and also between a person and his neighbor.*

When we read about *shalom* in Isaiah 53, we usually think particularly of the peace that individuals can have with God. But

Isaiah is thinking about society as well. Elsewhere he pictures a time when the Spirit will be poured out, when justice will live in the wilderness and the work of righteousness will be peace, and "my people will dwell in a habitation of *shalom*" (Isaiah 32:18, literal translation).

Nothing less than God's Spirit will bring about this large transformation. The Holy Spirit works towards *shalom* on a broad scale. It must have been this passage that led one Christian leader to conclude, "You can't have the Holy Spirit and work for war."

Shalom and war?

This language about *shalom* speaks to the question of war in the following ways. First, God's larger goal for his people, Israel, is *shalom*. But Israel was never only one ethnic group. Ruth, a Moabitess, Caleb the Kenizzite and Rahab the Canaanite became part of God's people. The prophets see large numbers of Gentiles joining God's people in the future (Amos 9.11-12; Isaiah 49.6). Further, God wants *shalom* not only for his own people, but also for all the people on earth (Zechariah 9:10).

Second, God gives peace because he is the source of peace. Wars come, as James explains, from human greed and sin (James 4:1-2). God, as we shall see later, is not outside the human tragedy of war, but his gift is peace.

The familiar benediction at the end of a church service begins, "The Lord bless you and keep you" and ends "the Lord lift up his countenance on you and give you peace" (Numbers 6:26). The Psalmist states, "The Lord blesses his people with peace" (Psalms 29:11). God offers *shalom*.

The way of peace follows directly from God's gift of peace. Approaching the question of war from the viewpoint of God's gift *(shalom)* and God's goal *(shalom),* we have to conclude that human warfare contradicts what God is about.

The statements about *shalom* must be read together with the reports of war in the Old Testament. When a person has to decide whether to participate in war today, on what basis will he or she decide—on the war reports or on the goal and vision for peace? Which of these is God's true, ultimate goal for human kind?

Given the whole story of God's dealings with the world from Genesis to Revelation, war is not the goal. On the grand scale of things, war is an "interim" activity. The ideal for believers is not something temporary but rather God's ultimate objective— *shalom.* Violence and destruction are contrary to God's larger purpose.

God says "no" to war

There are so many war stories in the Old Testament that the reader can miss the times when God says "no" to war.

An illustration of God's direct disapproval of war comes from the life of David. King David was a military king who fought numerous battles. Being a very religious man, he wanted to build a temple to honor the God whom he served. But the Lord didn't let David build the temple, for "You have shed much blood and have fought many wars. You are not to build a house in My Name because you have shed much blood on the earth in my sight" (1 Chronicles 22:8). David's military campaigns disqualified him.

In a related story God said "no" to trusting in military might. David tried to count his troops, against the advice of his commander Joab. It took him 10 months, and by that time he knew he had sinned. A prophet named Gad came in the name of God to offer him a choice between several forms of punishment (2 Samuel 24:13). David's sin was to rely on his army for security.

At the very least, these two examples show that war in the Old Testament did not have God's unqualified support. It is simply not true that God thirsts after war.

Don't bet on horses

More than once Isaiah warned Israel not to rely on military strength. One time Ahaz, king of Jerusalem, and his people feared an attack from two northern countries. Apparently Ahaz wanted to get help from Egypt. But Isaiah challenged him to trust in God alone, saying, "have firm faith or you will not stand firm" (Isaiah 7:9, NEB).

Isaiah also pronounced "woe" on Israel when they depended on Egypt for the military help of horses, their equivalent to the MX missile. God said their strength should lie in quietness and trust (Isaiah 30:1-2, 15-16).

The Psalmist wrote that military might is limited:

No king is saved by the size of his army;
No warrior escapes by his great strength.
A horse is a vain hope for deliverance;
Despite all its great strength, it cannot save (Psalm 33:16, 17).

These warnings against relying on military might do not rule out some form of participation in war, but they do give a perspective. Though God sends Israel to war at times, he also speaks against war at other times.

One more thing. Stories written among nations surrounding Israel often glorify war heroes. By contrast, except for Joshua, the Old Testament does not hold up war heroes for praise in the way that other nations do. Israel made no war monuments to commemorate victories over foes. Instead, they put up ten stones to mark the spot where God performed a miracle in leading them across the Jordan (Joshua 3:17-4:9).

Stories of peaceful living

War comes from tension and conflict. Self-defense, vengeance, differences of opinion, economic imbalances or uneven access to resources, and conflicting beliefs are the things that lead to war. But differences can be settled without war.

Abraham and Isaac provide examples of how explosive situations can be handled peacefully. Abraham's herdsmen had trouble getting along with Lot's herdsmen. Abraham's solution was to offer his nephew Lot the first choice of the most desirable grazing areas. Abraham was taking a risk, and it turned out that he ended up with the hilly area while his nephew took the lush Jordan valley (Genesis 13:5-11). He had the courage to surrender his rights in order to avoid conflict.

Isaac's story also involves a sticky situation. Two parties wanted the same waterholes. Abraham's servants had dug wells and apparently irrigated the area, making it productive. The envious Philistines closed one of the wells. When Isaac's servants reopened the well, the Philistines at Gerar quarreled with Isaac's herdsmen, claiming, "The water is ours." Isaac was rich and powerful and could have put those Philistines in their place. Instead he moved on and dug another well. Even when the Philistines harrassed him a second time, Isaac did not fight but moved on once more. Finally the Philistines stopped bothering him (Genesis 26:12ff.).

Did these patriarchs, Abraham and Isaac, perhaps understand better than modern "civilized" nations that war rarely settles anything?

Jeremiah preaches nonresistance

Jesus taught his followers, "do not resist an evil person." But long before Jesus walked the earth, Jeremiah preached nonresistance.

The world-conquering Babylonians were headed west, and Israel was just one more nation to conquer. Jeremiah advised Judah's kings not to resist the enemy (Jeremiah 27:11-12). Even worse, he told Zedekiah the king to *surrender* to the invading army.

It's not hard to guess what any patriotic Israelite would have thought of this suggestion. Government officials labelled Jeremiah a traitor, arrested him, and put him in a dungeon.

An unpopular position in the name of God and against government is sometimes necessary. In his day, Jeremiah represented a call for peace in the face of imminent destruction. Such a call is not unlike the modern call for peace in the face of communist advance or nuclear threat. Some have called Jeremiah the first pacifist.

Jeremiah, like Abraham and Isaac, wanted to meet the opposing party not with violence, but with peace. The rulers of his day didn't listen—and they perished.

There are voices for peace in the Old Testament, but you have to listen closely for them because they frequently get drowned out by stories of war. These voices tell us that God's ultimate goal is *shalom,* and that war is only an "interim" activity. They tell us that when people want to obey God, they will lay down their weapons and not learn war anymore. Can you hear the voices for peace?

Elmer A. Martens

Yahweh Fights His Own Kind of War

Bad news for King Jehoshaphat. A huge army of Moabites and Ammonites was on its way to attack Judah. Keeping his cool, the king told the whole country to fast, then gathered them together to ask the Lord what to do. The answer came through a Levite named Jahaziel: "Do not be afraid or discouraged because of this vast army. For the battle is not yours, but God's." On the day of the battle, Jehoshaphat asked a bunch of singers to lead the way. They praised the Lord for the splendor of his holiness. By the time the men of Judah reached the battlefield, "they saw only dead bodies lying on the ground; no one had escaped." The nations surrounding Judah were very impressed when they heard "how the Lord had fought against the enemies of Israel. And the kingdom of Jehoshaphat was at peace, for his God had given him rest on every side" (2 Chronicles 20).

The hard question of wars in the Old Testament must now be asked. There are certainly strong voices for war in the Old Testament. What are they saying? What are they trying to teach us? Let's listen.

In the Old Testament God is given several secondary titles. He is the "Good Shepherd" (Psalm 23), "Judge", "Law Giver" and "King" (Isaiah 33:22). Another striking description is "The Lord is a warrior."

That expression is found in a song sung after the great deliverance of the people of Israel from Egypt. After the Israelites were hastily sent off by the Pharaoh, they were soon followed by the Egyptian army.

God's people were trapped. In front of them was the Red Sea, on either side were mountains, and pursuing them from behind was the powerful Egyptian army. Their future looked grim.

The warrior at the Exodus

Then the unexpected, in fact the unimaginable, took place. The sea parted, and in the night God's people marched through on dry land. The Egyptians followed the Israelites into the parted sea, but then God covered the Egyptians, and they were destroyed.

The enemy had been wiped out; and the Israelites themselves had not as much as swung a sword or killed even one Egyptian. God as *warrior* had dealt effectively with the enemy—this time totally without Israel's help.

Safe on dry ground, the rejoicing Israelites broke into song, celebrating God's triumph. They were led by Miriam, Moses' sister. They sang:

I will sing to the Lord,
For He is highly exalted.
The horse and its rider
He has hurled into the sea.
The Lord is my strength and my song;
He has become my salvation,
He is my God and I will praise Him,
My father's God, and I will exalt Him.
The Lord is a warrior;
The Lord is His name (Exodus 15:1-3).

Israel had experienced the power of God. They had seen a warrior, greater than they could imagine, fight for them and win. This incident became a model. For centuries poets and prophets recalled the event with the message that Israel need not fight but must trust the Warrior Lord and obey Him.

This bold statement at the Exodus is not the only description of the warlike qualities of God. God uses a sword in Ezekiel 32:10 and Isaiah 34:6. Isaiah predicts that "The Lord will march out like a mighty man, like a warrior" (Isaiah 42:13). David gave thanks to God "who trains my hands for war, my fingers for battle" (Psalms 144:1).

His name is "Lord of Hosts"

In addition to these descriptions of God's war-like activity, there is a military expression used for God: *Yahweh Sebaoth,* usually translated "Lord of Hosts." The word *Sebaoth,* literally "armies or hosts," may refer to Israel's armies of which God is the leader (1 Samuel 17:45), or perhaps to heavenly beings such as angels (1 Kings 22:19), and sometimes to the sun, moon and stars (Deuteronomy 4:19).

The term Sebaoth is used 285 times in the Old Testament. It holds at least two major ideas: military might and majestic royalty. When Yahweh Sebaoth was used in connection with the nations, the term meant that God, the Lord of Hosts, was a total match for every power.

The term was also used in connection with worship, for example in Psalm 46:7-11. When Isaiah declared, "Holy, holy, holy, is the Lord of Hosts," he was in the temple (Isaiah 6:1). In worship settings, Yahweh Sebaoth had kingly authority, since he was in total command.

This explanation helps us understand what the Old Testament has in mind when it calls the Lord a man of war. It is referring to God's power. In Old Testament times strength and power were associated with a strong man, the warrior—just as we might associate those qualities with a fighter jet or MX missile.

The name Yahweh Sebaoth was a striking way of letting everyone know that God was the kingly strong man whose forces were equal to the opposing powers, whether nations or idols.

The warrior's enemies

The forces against which God fought were the forces of injustice. In the story of the Exodus, God's warrior activity was on behalf of oppressed people (Exodus 3:7-10). If he drove out the Canaanites, it was because of their sins. When nations exploited nations, God brought punishment, for example in Nahum 3:1.

While God often fought *for* Israel, sometimes he not only threatened but actually fought *against* Israel. Three examples are recorded: when the Israelites tried to take the land against God's will (Numbers 13:26-14:45); at Ai during the conquest (Joshua 7:1-5); and at Aphek against the Philistines (1 Samuel 4:1-11). These stories show that God does not always fight for a single national group—even his own people!

At one point the Assyrians were God's agent to punish Israel for injustice. But when Assyria became arrogant, God brought her to account by inciting other nations against her (Isaiah 10:12-19).

God's battles were not fought for a show of strength or delight in destruction. Quite the opposite—God has no pleasure in the death of persons (Ezekiel 33:11). In God's final battle when His enemies shall be destroyed in the great day of the Lord, his goal is the establishment of a kingdom of justice (Ezekiel 39:25-29).

God was and always will be a warrior God. There is a war that continues—the war between God and evil powers. God is a powerful warrior over the forces of evil and chaos symbolized by the monster Rahab (Isaiah 51:9-11). That same picture recurs in Revelation 6. From these passages we understand that evil will not gain the upper hand and that God will remain sovereign.

Calling people to war

As we listen to voices of war in the Old Testament, we hear God calling people to go to war. During the conquest, God said to Moses, "Treat the Midianites as enemies and kill them" (Numbers 25:17). Later in the book we read, "They fought against Midian as the Lord commanded Moses and killed every man" (31:7).

Bible readers have accounted for these and other similar passages in various ways. Some have said that a God who calls people to war could not be the same God who sent Jesus into the world. Others have said that Israel misunderstood God. Israel wanted to conquer territory and in order to justify war invoked the name of the Lord.

We must ask what God's reasons were for commanding war. An explanation for the expulsion of the Canaanites is given in Deuteronomy. God was not bringing Israel into the land of Canaan because Israel was a righteous people. No, "it is on account of the wickedness of these nations that the Lord is going to drive them out before you" (Deuteronomy 9:4-5). Wars were God's punishment on nations for their evil ways.

A second reason for the command to destroy the people of Canaan involved their evil influence. God ordered total destruction of the Hittites, Ammorites and others, "otherwise they will teach you to follow all the detestable things they do in worshipping their gods, and you will sin against the Lord your God" (Deuteronomy 20:17-18). Still other wars, such as those Gideon was called to fight, were for self-defense and security (Judges 6:14).

A helpful consideration is that Israel was both a people of God and a political group. One cannot simply say God commanded war in the past, therefore Christians today should also go to war. Individual Christians today belong to a nation, but Christians as a group do not make up a political group—they are part of every nation on earth.

The Lord's War

The most helpful observation about God's command to make war comes from looking at the kind of war which God commanded. The Bible describes this as the Lord's war (Numbers 21:14). Scholars in the past have called it a "Holy War." This war is quite unlike the wars we know.

The Lord's War had four characteristics which set it apart: religious ritual, charismatic leaders, victory though faith instead of military might, and the destruction of booty.

One *ritual* was to consult God before going into battle. The book of Judges reports civil war during which the people of Israel asked the Lord, "Shall we go up again to battle?" (20:23, 28). A threat in itself was not sufficient reason to go to war; the crucial question was,

"Does God approve?"

Another ritual before battle was to offer sacrifice. In Samuel's day the Philistine lords were on their way to fight Israel. Samuel offered a whole burnt offering as a call for help to the Lord (1 Samuel 7:9). Joshua called his people to offer sacrifice as an act of consecration before they entered the promised land (Joshua 3:5).

As a matter of course, soldiers were under certain hygienic restrictions that had nothing to do with military matters (Deuteronomy 23:9-14).

A more significant feature of the Lord's war was *leadership*. The person who addressed the army as it prepared for war was initially one of the priests, to be followed then by other officers (Deuteronomy 20:2). The priest, rather than military generals, would sometimes lead the way. The leader of the people at the Exodus was Moses, who is described not as a military general but as a prophet (Exodus 18:14-19).

The leaders for many of the Lord's wars were not military personnel; instead, they were people on whom God's Spirit had come—such as Gideon. The qualifications of a general seemed to have little or nothing to do with military expertise; and as for the "army", during the time of the judges these were farmers who often showed up with their farm tools.

Destroy the booty

One of the most interesting features of the Lord's war is that victory came not through military skill or strength in numbers or weapons, but as a result of *faith* in God. Nowhere is this better illustrated than in the familiar story of Gideon, whose initial army of 32,000 dwindled to 10,000 and then down to 300 (Judges 6-7).

In Gideon's war, the offensive weapons consisted of a pitcher, a torch and a trumpet. These "weapons" were hardly lethal! When victory came, it was not because of weapons or men but because of the intervention of the Almighty.

A fourth feature of the Lord's war was that as a rule the *booty* was to be dedicated to God. It was not to be taken for private or even public use. The city of Ai could not be conquered, the Scripture explains, because a man called Achan had failed to destroy all war booty. Achan was punished before the campaign could continue.

Another example comes from the life of King Saul. Saul's orders from God were to destroy the Amalekites completely but, as Saul explained to the prophet Samuel, the people wanted to keep some livestock. God's anger with Saul was great—and Saul's kingdom was taken from him (1 Samuel 15:28). This practice of complete destruction of booty was a safeguard against waging war for the sake of financial gain.

In view of these four characteristics of the Lord's war, it is not right to equate it with modern wars such as World War I or II. Modern wars are not waged from a sense of God's directive. Highly educated militarists, not religious leaders, direct the war effort. There is a constant demand for bigger armies and more lethal weapons. And the idea of the destruction of booty is unknown.

Lessons of the Lord's war

What did God intend to teach us through the war stories of the Old Testament?

First, God wanted to say that he enters the human scene and comes to the aid of troubled people. He is not a detached God. He entered the human scene according to the need and experience of the people. In their experience the warrior brought down the mighty. God is such a God.

Second, the stories show that God works by means other than the sword, such as miracles. At the Red Sea, the Israelites were exhorted, "The Lord will fight for you; you only need to be still" (Exodus 14:14). Indeed, Exodus 23:20-33 may suggest that God also intended Israel to conquer the land without using the sword. In that passage, God urges obedience, and promises that His angel will go before them and bring them into the land (verse 23); that His terror will precede Israel so that the land will be thrown into confusion (verse 27); or for that matter, that He will send hornets ahead of Israel to drive out the Hivites, Canaanites and Hittites before them (verse 28).

Third, these war stories help us understand faith. Consider what faith meant for the Israelite soldier going into the Lord's war, armed only with the promise that "The Lord shall fight for you." Imagine yourself as that soldier facing the deadly swords and spears of the enemy. To follow God now is to put your life on the line. Faith is a risk to the point of one's life that God will really come through.

Fourth, the Lord's wars show that God is sovereign and fully in control. He is Lord. Nobody is a match for him—not even the mighty empires of the Egyptians or Babylonians. That is the message the prophets picked up from these stories. When they recalled the events of the Exodus, for example, they declared that God had taken care of his and seen them through the most astonishing difficulties. If we follow him in obedience, we can trust him with our lives.

SHOULD A CHRISTIAN PARTICIPATE?

As we have noted in this and the previous chapter, the student of the Old Testament hears mixed voices. There are voices for peace and voices for war. Which voice should we listen to when we face the question whether a Christian should participate in war?

Our summary of the Old Testament teaching on peace and war must take into account the following observations:

The Old Testament teaching on war suggests a Christian's non-involvement. There is little doubt that the Exodus story—the first reported struggle involving a people group—is intended to be a model. In that conflict, Israel actively trusted God but did not lift up swords to kill. The emphasis on miracle is carried forward in the report of the Lord's wars during the time of the Judges, and in certain battles during the monarchy such as Jehoshaphat's battle and Hezekiah's contest with the Syrians.

The emphasis on God's unassisted role in victory is present later in the exilic time, when Daniel receives the vision of a huge statue representing world empires. The image is smashed by a rolling stone "cut without human hands."

Similarly, the emphasis on God as a warrior is introduced at the outset and continues through to Zechariah, one of the last prophets (see Zechariah 9). It is because God is a mighty warrior that the sword and spear are uncalled for.

Since the dominant note on war is sounded at the Exodus, we might think of the other types of war as concessions. In other words, God adjusted himself to the weakness of the people.

Could it be that the record of those other wars is given to show us how evil and unproductive wars are? The history of human wars, whether in the Old Testament or in any other history books, shows that war is a shame for humankind. War is ugly.

The Old Testament teaching on God's concern for life urges non-involvement in war. War is destructive and brings death. But the overall tone of the Old Testament is that God is concerned about life. He is the God who breathed into man the breath of life. As the giver of life, His intention is for *shalom.*

In light of ancient Near East culture, even some of the instructions about war have a human touch: "When you march up to attack a city, make its people an offer of peace....When you lay siege to a city for a long time...do not destroy its trees by putting an ax to them" (Deuteronomy 20:10, 19). Ezekiel announces, "as surely as I live, declares the sovereign Lord, I take no pleasure in the death of the wicked" (Ezekiel 33:11).

The high value placed on life is shown by the the direct command "thou shalt not kill" and by the severe penalty laid down for those who take life. Noah receives the directive "Whoever sheds the blood of man by man shall his blood be shed, for in the image of God has God made man" (Genesis 9:6).

The Old Testament teaching on peace calls for non-involvement in war. When deciding from the Old Testament whether to participate in war, the believer must ask "What is the direction in which God is moving?"

In the last chapter we noted the calls for peaceful living given in the book of Proverbs and illustrated in the stories of Abraham and Isaac and also in later incidents in Israel's life. The prophets picture a coming age of peace. They lift up our sights to a time when war will be no more, when conflict and destruction will be unknown.

Believers are God's advance agents of the coming kingdom. They have chosen to submit to God's ways. Since God's goal is *shalom,* these God-followers are committed to peaceful ways. The voices for peace in the Old Testament demand for today's Christian conscientious objection to war and non-participation in it.

The New Testament endorsement of the Old Testament pushes the believer toward non-participation in war. Jesus recognized that wars would continue in the world, yet he blessed the peacemakers. He taught that the one who fights with the sword will die by the sword. He called on his followers to love the enemy. To do so, even in the face of threat, is to follow up on the principles of the Lord's War and in trust leave the outcome to the Lord of Hosts.

Jesus' own example clinches the argument in favor of non-resistance. Suffering love and not revenge is the word from Jesus.

This call for peace is even stronger when we note that God's people are found not in one nation but in many nations. Who is to receive our first loyalty? The Old Testament answers, loyalty is above all to God, the Lord Sebaoth sovereign over nations. His people are different. They wage peace, not war.

John E. Toews

The Jesus Way in the Early Church

What just about drove the people from the synagogue crazy was the way his face looked like the face of an angel. They were already in a sweat over the great wonders and signs which Stephen did among the people, and whenever they'd tried to argue with him he'd beaten them hands down. So they'd arranged for false witnesses and had brought Stephen before the Jerusalem council. Stephen's defense was little more than a quick run-down of Jewish history, but his audience took issue with the punchline. They "ground their teeth against him," dragged him out of the city, and pelted him with rocks till he died. As the stones struck, Stephen first asked, "Lord Jesus, receive my spirit." Then he knelt down and prayed for his murderers, "Lord, do not hold this sin against them."

Jesus taught peace. The Old Testament taught peace. What happened to Jesus' teaching and example in the lives of his earliest followers, all of whom were Jewish students of the Old Testament? Did the disciple community founded by Jesus continue in his way or did it go in a different direction?

If the early church abandoned the Jesus way, then later generations of Christians could say that the Jesus way was too idealistic. But if the early church faithfully followed the way of Jesus, then Jesus' ethic is confirmed by those who were closest to him.

Resurrection and Pentecost

The early church saw itself as the disciple community of Jesus. It got this understanding from the resurrection of Jesus and the gift of the Holy Spirit at Pentecost.

The crucifixion raised questions about Jesus and his way. God answered all these questions in the resurrection. The resurrection meant that God put his stamp of approval on Jesus as Messiah and Lord. God made the crucified one Lord and Savior, Example and Leader.

The resurrection also meant Jesus was present in the life of his people. The community of disciples formed before the crucifixion could go on in the confidence that its leader and founder was indeed God's Messiah.

Pentecost made the reality of the resurrection even clearer. The risen Christ gave his people the gift of the Messianic Spirit which God's people had awaited for many centuries. Now they experienced what the resurrection meant, i.e., Jesus was Lord. He also was present among his people through his Spirit to give them what they needed to continue his mission in the world.

A missionary community from the start

The resurrection and Pentecost defined the church as the Jesus people in the world. This meant that the church was entrusted with the mission of the Kingdom of God which Jesus proclaimed. The church carried the Kingdom banner by proclaiming Jesus as Messiah and Lord.

In other words, the resurrection and Pentecost meant that the church was a missionary community from the start. It was a community proclaiming Jesus as Lord and calling people to enter the Kingdom community by accepting Jesus as Lord. It proclaimed salvation by faith and invited people to live the Jesus way as part of the church.

The church became the public display of the Jesus way. As Jesus people, the church is a visible community of God's people living in the world by the Jesus way. It is a minority community because it is for converted people only.

It is important to understand that in the Bible, peacemaking starts with the church. Biblical peacemaking is a project of the whole kingdom community. It is not just the stance of heroic individuals.

Jesus calls into being a new people, called the church, which is to embody the Jesus way on earth. It does so in the power of Jesus' resurrection and present Spirit and in anticipation of Jesus' ultimate reign over the entire universe.

SHAPE OF THE CHURCH'S PEACEMAKING

How does the church demonstrate the Jesus way in the world? What does the church's peacemaking look like? Here are several characteristics of the church's peacemaking style.

The church taught peacemaking

The church passed on the Jesus word about loving the enemy. In the earliest manuals of the church which were used to instruct new converts in the Jesus way, Jesus' command to love the enemy was placed in second position immediately after the beatitudes.

1 Thessalonians 5:15, Romans 12:14, 17-20 and 1 Peter 3:9 all teach Christians not to pay back evil for evil, but instead encourage positive action toward the enemy: "pursue good" in 1 Thessalonians; "bless," "be at peace with," and "feed" in Romans; "bless" in 1 Peter. The language and thought in each text is similar, which suggests that they all had Jesus' teaching in mind. The emphasis in each passage is on the positive action recommended.

The motive for loving the enemy is the salvation of God. In Romans the command is grounded in the mercies of God which Christians are to reflect, while in 1 Peter the reason is "you were called to this in order that you might inherit a blessing." Christian faith that does not express itself in love for the enemy is denied the blessing of God.

The command to love the enemy was a hard one for the early church. The enemy was no longer the oppressor of Jewish national dreams, but the unbelieving persecutor of Christians—the hostile family members or neighbors and local officials who treated the members of the church badly.

The command seemed unjust. The enemy who scorned God and mistreated God's people did not deserve blessing, the Christians tended to think. To give their backing to this hard command, both Peter and Paul supported the teaching of Jesus with quotations from the Old Testament. The love command summed up the Old Testament for Paul and Peter just as it did for Jesus. And the love command expresses itself in loving the enemy, in feeding, in doing good toward and in blessing the persecutors and opponents of the church.

The Christian is not just passive in the face of evil and violence. Rather, he or she is an active peacemaker who overcomes evil by deeds of love and kindness.

The church imitated Jesus

When the letters of the New Testament talk about discipleship, they talk about imitating Christ. Check, for example, Romans 6:6-11 and 15:1-7; Galatians 2:20; Colossians 1:24 and 2:12-3.1; Philippians 2:3-14 and 3:10ff.; 2 Corinthians 4:10 and 8:7-9; Ephesians 5:25-28; 1 Peter 2:20ff.; 1 John 2:6.

These texts make it clear that the Christian is to follow Christ in his expression of love, sacrifice, giving, death and resurrection. The follower of Jesus is a servant, not a boss; a forgiver, not a hothead. Christians are to love and serve each other as Christ loved and served them. Christians also are to suffer willingly rather than inflict suffering.

In other words, the disciple style in the world is the style of the cross. The disciple's reward for the cross is the resurrection just as it was for Jesus. Again, the church is a peacemaking community within itself and in its relation to the world.

A community of reconciled enemies

Baptism into Christ changes all relationships, states Galatians 3:27ff. It breaks down the walls between Greek and Jew, slave and free, and male and female in Christ. These three pairs identify the three deepest divisions of ancient society. Such divisions have no place, Paul asserts, in the thought and practice of those who are united with Christ.

Here as in 1 Corinthians 12:12ff. and Colossians 3:9-11 Paul states that baptism into Christ reconciles. Baptism into the Christian church destroys the barriers that separate people in the world. Within the Jesus community former enemies are reconciled—they live in peace as brothers and sisters in Christ.

Paul makes a similar point in Ephesians 2:11ff. Christ creates an alternative society, the church. He is praised in verses 14-18 for bringing two enemy peoples together. The peace Christ brings is peace in society—it reconciles enemy people into a new community. The oneness Christ creates disrupts all popular ways of thinking and relating because it is a brand new way of being together in the world. Paul calls this new reality "the new man" and "the house of God," and in 5:23-32 he identifies this new man as the church.

Notice how this new public reality is described as an act of creation. It is not a remodeled old reality, but something new which God creates. If you compare this creation account with the creation story in Genesis you will notice something interesting. In Genesis man is the last creature created. Here the new man is created first.

The church is the "first fruits"—the first pick of the coming harvest—of God's creation in Christ. The rest of creation waits for the liberation and reconciliation which is to come to the world through the church as it demonstrates the Jesus way.

Paul uses the word "peace" four times in Romans 14-15 (14:17, 19; 15:13, 33). There is conflict in the churches at Rome over questions of food and ethnic background. Paul exhorts the members of the church to live in peace by welcoming different kinds of people and by giving up personal rights so that other Christians can grow.

The point Paul makes is that the church is to be a peacemaking community within itself. Christ has removed the hatred that normally divides people, he has modeled self-giving love for others, and he is creating a new kind of peacemaking people in the world.

Jesus is Lord

The early church distinguished itself by a lifestyle that did not conform to the way most people lived. It showed this nonconformist style most clearly by rejecting Caesar's way—asserting oneself and making oneself a god. Caesar's way symbolized the values of pagan Roman society. The early Christians chose Jesus as Lord rather than Caesar. They rejected the most fundamental symbol of their society. The price for their stance often was death.

The early church was courageously nonconformist because it believed that Christ had defeated and triumphed over "the principalities and powers." Paul used the word "powers" for civil authorities, but by "principalities and powers" Paul mainly meant the spiritual powers that stood behind and acted through the civil governments. They are supernatural and demonic powers who control the universe and society.

These powers, Paul says, acted together to defeat Christ. Christ submitted himself to them and defeated them in death and triumphed over them in the resurrection. Paul describes this triumph in different ways—Christ abolished the slavery of the powers, he disarmed the powers, he made a public example of them—but the different words mean the same thing: Christ has broken the reign of the powers and has set the believer free from their grasp (see Romans 8:38; Ephesians 3:10 and 6:12; Colossians 1:16 and 2:25).

One of the confessions that the early Christians used together was "Jesus is Lord." By that they meant that he was Lord of the world because he had defeated the powers which formerly controlled the world. Christians were free to obey Christ rather than Caesar. Therefore, they weren't afraid to die for nonconformity. Christ had defeated death. The state's ultimate means of social control, the death penalty, had lost its meaning. Jesus had robbed the state of the power of force by his own death and resurrection.

Unafraid of the government, the early Christians were liberated to live the Jesus way. That meant nonconformity in the world—Jesus' way rather than Caesar's way.

THE MESSAGE OF ROMANS 13

If you have followed the discussion this far, there is one text you might want to ask, What about Romans 13? Does Paul not teach Christians to obey the state, including the state's demand to use force and violence in the defense or advance of its rights?

Few Scripture passages have been as misunderstood and misused as Paul's comments in Romans 13. From the time of the Roman Emperor Constantine in the early fourth century to the present, this text has been understood by most Christians as a call to obey the demands of the state. The government, it has been argued, has been ordained by God.

This understanding has been challenged in our time by the crisis of Nazism. The German Church's cooperation with Hitler during World War II has led many Christians to study this passage in detail once more. Now a different interpretation of Romans 13 is gaining wide acceptance among Bible teachers and church leaders.

Nonresistance toward the government

Romans 13 is part of a larger passage which starts with Paul's exhortation in 12:1ff.: "be not conformed...so that you may discern the will of God."

The more specific passage is about leaving vengence to God while practicing suffering love (12:14ff.). Christians are not to repay evil with evil, but are to live in peace and out of a love which will not hurt the neighbor.

In 49 A.D. the Emperor Claudius forced all Jews out of Rome for political activity which the Roman government viewed as dangerous. When the Jews were allowed to come back five years later, they returned to the city in anger. Many Jews, including Jewish Christians, wanted to revolt against Rome.

Paul, writing to the churches in Rome only six month to two years following the return of Jews to the city, sensed the situation was so explosive that he addressed it in his letter. The focus of his comments was that Christians should be nonresistant in their stance toward the government.

Secondly, Paul defines the government as "the powers" (13:1). That term refers to both the civil authorities and the spiritual powers behind them. This understanding of government leads Paul to a mixed attitude toward it. On the one hand, it has a positive role. On the other hand, it is a temporary institution. Therefore, Christians must be critical of the state, while obeying it as long as it remains within its bounds.

Thirdly, Paul does not say in verses 1 and 2 that God ordained the powers that be. The Greek word here means to put them in order. God did not ordain or bless the powers. He simply orders them—he brings them into line with his purposes. Paul's message to Christians tempted with revolutionary action is, "be subordinate, because the state is ordered by God."

Fourthly, the job of government, according to verses 3-7, is to reward good and evil according to their merits. Not everything a government does or asks of its citizens is good. Paul states that the activity of government can be tested. Does it consistently reward good and evil according to their merits?

Measure the claims of Caesar

Verse 7 points clearly to this kind of testing. This verse is probably the earliest commentary on Jesus' words in Mark 12:17: "Render to Caesar the things that are Caesar's, and to God the things that are God's." Paul says that Caesar is to be given back the coins stamped with his image, but earlier (12:1ff.) he stated that we are to give to God that which is stamped by his image—our whole lives.

Paul goes on to list what belongs to Caesar and what belongs to God: taxes, custom and honor to Caesar, but "fear" only to God. So the command "to render to all what is due them" does not mean "render to the state everything asked." The task of the state is limited to governing justly. The duty of the Christian is limited to taxes and honor.

Paul wants to see Christians test or "discern" the ethics of the government. The "render to each his due" of verse 7 is defined in verse 8 as "nothing is due to anyone except love." *The claims of Caesar are to be measured by the claims of love.* Love, in turn, is defined in verse 10 as that which does no harm.

Fifthly, the obligation to the state which is demanded in verse 1 does not mean obedience in the strict sense. Paul avoids using the three normal Greek words for obedience. These words mean a complete bending of one's will to the desires or demands of another. Instead Paul uses a word that means "to be subordinate to" or "to stand under."

Stand under government; obey God

Paul calls Christians to be subordinate, but not to be obedient. The Christian who refuses to do what the government commands, but remains under its authority, is being subordinate even though he is not obeying. Subordination involves a serious and responsible disobedience whenever obedience to the government would involve disobeying God. It makes room for obedience to God rather than men where the two claims to loyalty are in conflict.

Finally, the sword in Romans 13 is not the sword of battle or execution, but the smaller dagger carried by Roman authorities as the symbol of their civil authority. Romans 13, therefore, does not call the Christian to use the sword, but rather to recognize the state's authority to reward good and evil according to their merits.

Romans 13 does not say whether it is acceptable or not for the government to use force. Rather it calls Christians to a nonconformist and nonresistant stance in the world. Christians are not to take up arms for or against the government.

This nonresistant understanding of Romans 13 was practiced in the life of the early church for the first 300 years of church history. The early church understood itself as a peacemaking community in its relation to the government until the time of Constantine in the early fourth century.

Victory of the Warrior Lamb

The final book of the New Testament, Revelation, paints a colorful picture of Christian peacemaking. The church is being persecuted. Some Christians are despairing; others think it is time to join the Zealots and fight the injustices of Roman rule.

The risen Christ appears and says, "do not be afraid..." (1:17). Why? Because Christ is the Victor. He is the Lion who triumphs over all enemies, all kings, all principalities and powers.

But then the surprise. The Lion is really "a Lamb with the marks of slaughter on him" (5:6). In scenes that are filled with holy war images from the Old Testament, Jesus is presented as a warrior who is different. He does battle with the principalities and powers, not human beings. He defeats and disarms the powers by suffering and death. Christ the Warrior of God wins by being killed, not by killing. God raises him, subjects all things to him and enthrones him as King of kings and Lord of lords.

The church is called to suffer with the Warrior Lamb, not to fight for him or any of the kings of the earth. The role of the Christian is to wait patiently and to suffer faithfully for the final victory of the battle the Warrior Lamb won at Calvary. The Christian makes peace by suffering with his or her Lord because he or she knows the Warrior Lamb triumphed in self-giving love.

Reverse fighting

The early church followed Jesus' plan for a new way of togetherness. That way determines the church's inner life and its relationship to the world. On the inside it means the church teaches and imitates Jesus in his way of reconciliation in place of hostility and fighting, his way of servanthood in place of lordship. On the outside, in relating to the world, the church is nonconformist, nonresistant and a peacemaker.

The New Testament way of peacemaking means the church rejects violence in all relationships —within the disciple community, between the disciple community and the world, and between members of the disciple community and individuals in the world. But the church does more than reject. *It replaces violence with a way of love, servanthood and peacemaking.*

Christ and his people are peacemakers. They fight, but it is "reverse fighting." They fight by loving, giving and dying—never by violence and killing.

Jesus is the way to life and the way to live. Jesus demonstrates a new way of living before God in the world. The church is the present display of the Jesus way in the world. The Jesus way is love and peacemaking.

John Fast

Christian Responses toward War and Peace

William Penn's "Holy Experiment" in Pennsylvania provided a notable exception to the way in which Europeans enslaved and murdered Indians during their colonization of North and South America. The Quakers attempted to establish a colony where justice and friendliness toward the Indians could be pursued peaceably. Penn always considered the native Americans as equals and was the only governor who actually bought and consistently paid the market price for his settlers' land. His peace treaties with Indians are legendary. Church historian Roland Bainton considers Penn's experiment the finest example of the treatment of natives to be found in history.

One of the most important ethical issues today is the Church's response to war and peace. The Church has wrestled with this question for 2,000 years. We can learn a great deal from that history.

The Christian Church has held three main views of war and peace since the time of Christ. Pacifism was the prevalent conviction of the early church. After the emperor Constantine declared Christianity the religion of the Roman empire in 313 A.D., the church saw its role in trying to curb the excesses of violence. It came up with the theory of a "just war."

After justifying existing wars the Church began to endorse new wars. The third type of response from the Church was the "holy war." Crusades were led by the Christian Church during the Middle Ages. The Church thought of itself as God's tool to stamp out infidels and pagans.

Since the Protestant Reformation of the 16th century, these three responses—pacifism, just war and crusade—have continued in various combinations. The failure of two world wars to curb international conflict and the birth of the nuclear age have caused modern Christians to re-examine their attitudes toward war and peace.

The early church was pacifist

The previous chapter showed how the New Testament Church took Jesus at his word about peace. Most scholars agree that in the years that followed, the early Church interpreted Jesus Christ as a peacemaker and themselves as pacifists.

Tertullian, an early Church father, defended pacifism by stating that love and killing are incompatible. He thought that it was "better to be killed than to kill."

Origen, responding to a critic of Christianity, stated that "Jesus did not consider it compatible with his inspired legislation to allow the taking of human life in any form at all." An early Church instruction manual states that a "soldier of civil authority must be taught not to kill men and to refuse to do so if he is commanded."

Another church father, Cyprian, noted that murder by individuals is considered a crime; and yet public killing by an army is seen as a virtue. He maintained that God had designed "iron for tilling, and not for killing."

All the evidence shows that the policy of the early Church was to return good for evil and to conquer evil with good. No major Christian leaders before Constantine's reign justified the participation of believers in warfare.

The early Church refused to participate in war for three reasons. First and foremost was its concern to be obedient to Jesus. Second, early church leaders recognized that obedience to Jesus was impossible for a soldier, because he was required to obey the emperor. Third, the early Christians were guided by the hope that God's will would win in the end even though they endured persecution and martyrdom. This hope of victory freed them from conformity to the world.

Christians enter the army

Although there were Christians in the army by 180 A.D., there were never many. Soldiers were almost never mentioned in reports of early Christian vocations. But the trend was slowly changing. Why?

During the *Pax Romana* (Roman Peace) the army functioned largely as a civil service and police force. Some Christians entered this non-combatant role. People also were becoming more loyal to the empire, particularly when they weren't persecuted as much. Therefore we see evidence for Christian participation in the military increasing after 180 A.D.

The teachings of the early Church theologians continued to disapprove of believers serving in the army. The early Church's disciplinary measures forbade converts to enter the forces. If a new convert was already in the army, however, he was allowed to stay, provided he did not kill anyone. Those who violated these rules were excommunicated from the church.

The early Church was clearly pacifist in its teachings and practice. Pacifism has not been the dominant view in Christian thinking since those first centuries, however. To understand the reasons for that shift we must examine the development of a "Christian Roman Empire" under Constantine.

The "just war" in a Christian Roman Empire

The pacifism of the early Church developed at a time when the Roman government and culture were hostile to it. The Roman Empire tried to take charge of both religious and secular areas of life, and even demanded that all citizens worship the emperor. For disobeying that order the early Christians were accused of treason and disloyalty.

All this changed when Emperor Constantine became a Christian in the fourth century. He proclaimed Christianity the religion of the empire, and proclaimed himself chief bishop of the Church. As a result, the persecution of Christians ended—but so did the dominance of pacifism as a Christian attitude toward war.

Most Christians thought the golden age had arrived with Constantine in the form of a "Christian Roman Empire." It no longer made sense to resist the state and suffer persecution. Rather, they began to support Constantine's effort to place the entire empire under the Christian banner. This support included fighting the emperor's wars. By the fifth century *only* Christians could serve in the army.

To justify this new position the Church had to revise its theory of war. It borrowed heavily from the writings of the classical thinkers Plato and Cicero, but it was Augustine, Bishop of Hippo (354-430 A.D.), who formulated the "just war" theory in its Christian form. For Augustine a war was just if it was fought for just reasons and in a just manner.

The "just war" theory is dealt with in a later chapter of this book. How did it function in the fourth century? One illustration of its use occurred in 390 A.D. when Emperor Theodosius I ordered the deliberate massacre of 7,000 people in the city of Thessalonica. Ambrose, Bishop of Milan, ordered the emperor to do public penance for this unjustified act of atrocity. Theodosius finally obeyed the bishop, demonstrating that an emperor's political actions were subject to the moral scrutiny of the Church.

An interesting concession was made to pacifism, however. Monasticism emerged during the Middle Ages as a renewal movement in the church. It taught that ministers (priests) took vows of celibacy, poverty and obedience, and were prohibited from military service. Regular Christians could participate in marriages, fight in just wars, engage in farming or other civic functions. Only a few were called to true spirituality, which included pacifism. The Church's acceptance of monasticism implied that true Christians should not fight wars.

Killing unbelievers

The "just war" theory led quickly to the crusades of the 11th century.

An attempt was made in 1054 to promote the "Peace of God and the Truce of God." The "Peace of God" decreed that clergy, women, pilgrims, peasants and others were off limits to "just war" fighters, and the "Truce" declared that no fighting was allowed on certain holy days.

Peace militias were formed under the umbrella of the Church to enforce this peace, but their campaigns failed to stem the fighting and bickering of various groups in Europe.

Pope Urban II then urged the Council of Clermont in 1095 to fight the Turks. Since they were fighting Turks, and not Christians, the normal rules of the just war did not have to apply. Fighting them became a sacred cause.

For the first time in the history of Christianity the Church actually started wars. A favorite battle cry was a verse from Jeremiah: "Cursed be he that keepeth back his hand from blood." And these crusades were bloody. Raymond of Agiles described the capture of Jerusalem in this graphic way: "Men rode in blood up to their knees and the bridle reins. Indeed it was a just and splendid judgment of God, that this place should be filled with the blood of the unbelievers. ...The Lord made this day, and we rejoiced and exulted in it, for on this day the Lord revealed himself to His people and blessed them."

Even the formerly pacifist clergy formed monastic military orders such as the Templars and the Hospitalers. They were encouraged by St. Bernard to "attack with confidence and courage the enemies of the cross of Christ."

These religious crusades were also used to stamp out heresy within the church. A movement called the Cathari sprang up in southern France. These people did not believe in war and strongly rejected the authority of the Church. A brutal inquisition followed. Frenchmen were drafted with an offer of pardon for sins from the church to stamp out this heresy. In the town of Beziers, a Papal representative was asked how to distinguish Catharis from Catholics. His reply was, "Kill them all; God will know which are his."

CHRISTIAN RESPONSES SINCE THE REFORMATION

As long as the church was unified, it responded uniformly to the issue of war and peace. But when the church divided at the Reformation, Christian responses to war diversified. The interpretations, however, essentially remain variations of pacifist, just war and crusade convictions.

One factor in the plurality of Christian approaches has been the changing relationship between church and state. The Reformation of the early 16th century undermined the pope's domination of both civil and political life, and separated church and state authority.

The rise of nation-states which followed left the church with very little to say regarding the morality of the state's decisions, particularly as they related to war. In fact, many larger Protestant denominations were defined by their national boundaries. England was Anglican, Germany became Lutheran, Geneva turned Reformed and Spain remained Roman Catholic. In the 16th century, religious liberty was defined by the freedom to practice the religion of one's country, not the religion of one's choice.

A second factor in the diversification of responses to war has been the changing nature of warfare and violence. Wars of religion in Europe differ from the extermination of native peoples during the colonization of North America. Responses to two global wars of the 20th century differ from Christian reactions to the present threat of nuclear annihilation. And many are beginning to understand the spiral of violence that results in starvation for three-quarters of the earth's inhabitants—a more insidious form of warfare that claims more lives than open conflicts.

Luther, Calvin and wars of religion

The clash between Catholicism and Protestantism stood at the heart of many of Europe's religious wars. After Martin Luther was banned from the Catholic church and empire in 1521, the conflicts continued almost non-stop, culminating with the Thirty Years' War in Germany (1618-48).

Spain resumed its Inquisition, the pope declared another crusade against the Turks, Luther reacted to the peasants' war, Ulrich Zwingli lost his life leading Reformed Protestants to battle against Swiss Catholics, and John Calvin restored the ideal of a holy commonwealth in Geneva by endorsing a series of crusades against the Catholics. When the futile Thirty Years' War had ended, three fifths of Germany's 16 million people were killed.

Martin Luther typified the just war response. According to Luther, wars were the logical extension of the state's police function to prevent chaos in order that the Word of God could be freely proclaimed. Every human occupation became a way of loving God by loving your neighbor—even the jobs of jurists, hangmen and soldiers. One of the duties of a Christian prince, for Luther, was to repel invaders and defend his territory.

Luther considered it an act of love to kill, rob and pillage the enemy until one had conquered him. However, both princes and soldiers must fulfill certain just-war guidelines, drawn primarily from the Old Testament and the common wisdom of Luther's day.

Calvin replaced the central Lutheran idea of love with the notion of God's majesty. According to Calvin, the "glory of God" was superior to the claims of brotherly love. He repeatedly stated that no consideration could be paid to humanity when the honor of God was at stake.

Calvin was willing to employ any means, including burning heretics, planning assassinations and entering wars, in order to "ward off harm" and "preserve order." He saw all these as fitting into the larger purpose of glorifying God.

Murder and slavery

During Christopher Columbus' first trip to the "New World" in 1492 he wrote in his diary: "The Indians from the Antilles were cordial, kind, open-hearted, curious, intelligent." In the same diary Columbus, who called himself "bearer of Christ," prayed to God that above anything else he be allowed to find gold!

Thus began the systematic murder and exploitation of Indian peoples. The English, Spanish, French and Dutch dominated North and South America by despotic and oppressive rule. Where they did not actually kill the Indians, they subjected them to the most horrible servitude.

Spanish Catholics attempted to justify their invasions in 1513 by announcing a set of conditions which the Indians were forced to follow if they wanted to avoid war. The natives were to acknowledge the Church as the ruler of the world and the king of Spain as its representative. The terms could not be understood by the Indians.

New England Puritans viewed their conquest of the natives as a crusade commanded by God. They identified themselves as the new Israel out to conquer the promised land of Canaan. They enslaved and murdered Indians.

William Penn and the Pennsylvania Quakers provided a notable example of a pacifist response to colonization, described at the beginning of this chapter. Although only moderately successful, the Quakers succeeded in being more democratic than most other colonies. They also kept the death penalty to a minimum, made prisons more humane and avoided official sanction of war as long as they remained the majority in the Pennsylvania legislature.

Global conflicts

World War I was a new kind of war—one which involved the whole globe. What was the role of the Christian church in rallying mass support to accept and fight such a war?

Both the Catholic and Protestant churches of Germany justified the war on grounds of self-defense. Germany believed herself strangled by the nations around her. The churches of England took a more crusading spirit. The Bishop of London rallied the young British soldiers:

Kill Germans—to kill them, not for the sake of killing, but to save the world, to kill the good as well as the bad, to kill the young men as well as the old, to kill those who have shown kindness to our wounded as well....As I have said a thousand times, I look upon it as a war for purity, I look upon everyone who dies in it as a martyr.

When the United States entered the war, it was under the banner "to make the world safe for democracy." Church leaders of most denominations united to interpret W.W. I as a holy war—a war fought on behalf of God.

The only churches who did not take this approach were the various peace denominations. The majority of Quaker and Mennonite men drafted for the war remained true to nonresistance and faced imprisonment or were court-martialed. Some accepted alternative and non-combatant service.

Shallow pacifism rejected

World War I was to have been a war to end all wars. But when it was over many people realized that wars cause more problems than they solve. Many churches resolved never to bless another war and pacifism became very popular during the 1920s and 30s. However, this pacifism fell into disrepute among more conservative churches in the 1930s because they associated it with liberalism, and it evaporated completely when the League of Nations failed to contain Nazism. After Japan attacked Pearl Harbor many former pacifists began supporting the U.S. entry into W.W. II. They considered the war the fastest way to establish peace.

Once the world had witnessed the mass incinerations of Hamburg, Dresden, Auschwitz, Dachau and Tokyo and then were numbed by the dropping of atomic bombs on Hiroshima and Nagasaki, the "search for true peace through war" lost its meaning. The dropping of the bomb by the U.S. on August 6, 1945 signalled the start of the mad race toward nuclear annihilation. Could Christians ever justify war again?

Spiral of modern violence

Modern violence can be briefly described as a spiral with three main stages:

Violence in the system. The arms race is a form of "systemic" violence because it kills even without war. The world's military budget absorbs $1.3 million of the public treasure *every minute of the day,* while 30 children die every minute for want of food and medicine.

Subversive violence. The poor and disenfranchised take to the streets or the hills and become terrorists, guerrillas or freedom fighters (depending on who labels them). They feel they have no option but to resort to armed conflict.

Repressive violence. People in power react to revolution by creating secret police systems, using torture, and making existing institutions even more repressive.

How have the churches responded to modern violence? It is a sign of hope that many Christians are attempting to face the real issues of violence in our age. Because the nuclear threat is the most visible obstacle to peace for North Americans, many churches have taken the "nuclear pacifist" position. They are applying the just-war criteria to this new form of threatened warfare and have declared it a sin.

The doctrine of deterrence, or the threatened use of nuclear weapons, has been the U.S. defense policy since W.W. II. It is essentially a "peace through strength" policy. Churches which tend to identify their faith with nationalistic goals support deterrence. Other Christians believe that national security is meaningless without global peace. They have committed themselves to a more biblical vision of peace, and have created aggressive ministries that work at various levels for nonviolent change.

Mervin Dick

The Story of the Anabaptists

Under cover of darkness, a group of about a dozen men trudged slowly through the streets of Zurich to the home of Felix Manz. There they spent time in prayer asking God to guide them and to give them courage to do his will. They rose from their knees to take one of the most decisive actions in the history of the Christian Church. George Blaurock, a former priest, walked over to Conrad Grebel and asked Grebel to baptize him in the biblical manner, based on his personal confession of faith in Jesus Christ. Without hesitation, Grebel baptized him. George Blaurock then baptized all the others in the group. This small group of people gave birth to an important expression of the Protestant Reformation, called Anabaptism.

The Protestant Reformation of the early 16th century was one of the great dividing lines in the history of the Christian Church. Most of what we see in the Christian Church today has its roots in the Protestant Reformation.

The central figure of the Reformation was Martin Luther, a Roman Catholic monk and professor of theology at Wittenburg in Germany. Under his leadership a new form of church, known as Protestant, came into being. If we want to understand the Anabaptist way of peace, we have to go back to Luther.

Although many factors contributed to the Reformation, its basic cause was a spiritual one. In one sense it began as a personal struggle for Martin Luther. He had a brilliant mind, a deep devotion to God and the best education of his time. Yet he was restless because he wasn't sure of his own salvation.

Luther felt he was a doomed sinner. No amount of penance or soothing advice from his friends could satisfy the young monk's distress. So he gave himself to the intense study of the Scriptures.

In the year 1515 Luther's study led him to a revolutionary new understanding of God and his dealings with people. Romans 1:17 became the key which unlocked Luther's heart and mind. When he read "the just shall live by faith" he came to understand that "through grace and sheer mercy God justifies us through faith."

Salvation through faith

This was a startling revelation for the troubled Luther. The result was a conversion experience; he felt himself "to be reborn and to have gone through open doors into paradise." He saw clearly now that the cross of Jesus Christ alone removed human sin and became the way of reconciliation with God. Luther had come to his famous doctrine of "justification by faith." He had found peace at last!

This understanding of salvation clashed sharply with the teaching of the Roman Catholic Church. The church held that justification with God came by faith together with good deeds. Favor with God came from accepting church teachings and participating faithfully in the ritual of the church. Luther's new discovery, founded on the Scriptures alone, was that only faith was necessary for salvation.

Luther's discovery had far-reaching consequences. It challenged the church of his time to the core. With increased intensity Luther criticized the practices of the church as being corrupt and in need of correction. Finally, Luther prepared a list of 95 statements of belief which he nailed to the door of the church in Wittenburg on October 31, 1517. These 95 theses became the foundation upon which the Protestant churches of our time have been built.

Luther's action and his continued disagreement with the church, its bishops and the pope, led to the circulation of a document from the pope which condemned Luther and called him a "wild boar" who "had invaded the Vineyard." He was declared a heretic and eventually excommunicated from the church. But the die was cast. A new form of the church was born. And it grew rapidly.

Bible studies in Zurich

While Luther was forming his new theology in Germany, changes were also taking place in the city of Zurich, Switzerland. In 1519 a new priest by the name of Ulrich Zwingli was appointed to the Great Munster Church there. His method of reforming the church was through the preaching of powerful, biblical sermons. His messages were fresh and vigorous as he preached through whole books of the Bible, chapter by chapter.

Over a period of time Zwingli and the City Council of Zurich overturned one Catholic practice and doctrine after another. The change which made the greatest impact was ending the Catholic Mass in 1525 and replacing it with the biblical Lord's Supper.

Zwingli held Bible classes with students who were interested in studying the Scriptures for themselves. Among these students was a young man named Conrad Grebel. During his student days Grebel had lived a wild and undisciplined life. But under the influence of Zwingli and his Bible studies, Grebel had a conversion experience which changed him completely.

For about a year Grebel was excited about the changes Zwingli was making in the church. Then his attitude began to change. Grebel felt that Zwingli was too cautious about reform efforts. It bothered him that Zwingli referred final decisions about changes in the church to the City Council. This was wrong, Grebel believed, because it gave political rulers the authority to make spiritual decisions. He believed that the only basis for ordering church life was the Scriptures. Disagreement began to grow between Zwingli with his followers and Grebel with his supporters.

Conrad Grebel and the faithful church

At the very center of this disagreement was a difference of belief concerning the nature of the church. For Zwingli, church and political authority were closely linked. Both Zwingli and Luther considered all those who lived in a particular geographical area to be Christian and therefore part of the church. The old concept of the state church had not ended with the Reformation.

Grebel believed that the Church should be made up only of those who voluntarily followed Jesus Christ, regardless of geographical or political boundaries. The faithful Church, as Christ intended it to be, he said, orders its life and practice on the Scriptures. It is separate and distinct from all political authority. Obedience to Christ and his teaching is the primary concern of the Church.

The issue that led to the parting of ways for Zwingli and Grebel was baptism. Zwingli continued to practice baptism of infants. Conrad Grebel and a small group of other people could find no biblical basis for this. They could find in the New Testament only one basis for baptism, conversion. In the early church only men and women who had experienced personal spiritual conversion to Christ were fit subjects for baptism. So they tried to persuade Zwingli to give up the practice of infant baptism. But under pressure from the City Council, Zwingli refused.

Finally the Council warned all parents to have their infants baptized or face banishment from the territory. A few days later, on January 21, 1525, the Council ordered Grebel and Felix Manz to stop holding Bible classes. What would these believers who found no biblical basis for infant baptism do? They met that evening to decide, and the result was the secret baptismal service described at the beginning of this chapter.

Anabaptist means "rebaptizer." In fact, these early brethren did not practice rebaptism. They simply practiced baptism as they were convinced the Scriptures taught. Mennonites today, including the Mennonite Brethren Church, are the spiritual descendants of these early Anabaptists.

Missionary spirit of the Anabaptists

Insisting on adult baptism was a costly step for these dedicated men to take. Soon they were driven from the church in Zurich. But this did not hinder Grebel and his fellow believers. They were so filled with enthusiasm and a desire to share the good news of Jesus Christ that they began to journey throughout that region as traveling evangelists. Many persons responded to this missionary effort, and the newly-formed church grew rapidly.

All of this proved a serious threat to Zwingli and his church. Conrad Grebel was arrested, tried and sentenced to life imprisonment. Somehow, he managed to escape from prison. But the experience proved costly to Grebel's health and led to his death from the plague in the summer of 1526.

Felix Manz was arrested and placed in prison. Several times he was set free, only to be arrested again and imprisoned. Finally on January 5, 1527, he was bound hand and foot and drowned in the Limmat River in Zurich.

George Blaurock was arrested, tortured and burned to death. As he died he held up his fingers in a manner prearranged with his friends to indicate that he was still trusting in Christ.

Within two and a half years of the founding of this new church, its primary founders were all dead. Faithfully following Jesus and being a part of his true church was costly for them.

But the Anabaptist movement could not be stopped. The movement soon became visible in South Germany as well as Switzerland. The leaders in this area were Hans Denck, Hans Hut, Balthasar Hubmaier, Pilgram Marpeck and Michael Sattler. Their teaching and preaching drew the opposition of both the traditional state church and the Roman Catholic Church. The persecution that followed was intense. Only Hans Denck, who died of the plague, and Pilgram Marpeck, who held a prominent position as a civil engineer, escaped martyrs' deaths.

Conversion of a Dutch priest

The movement also spread to the Netherlands. There it took two different directions. Melchior Hoffmann, the leader who brought the movement to Holland, had a symbolic rather than literal approach to understanding the Bible. He also had great interest in the biblical books of Daniel and Revelation.

One group of his followers became violent and unbalanced under the leadership of Jan Matthijs. This group later attempted to establish in the city of Munster an earthly kingdom patterned after Old Testament life, under a man named Jan of Leiden. This fanatical movement ended in a bloody armed conflict with the army of the state church.

There was also a peaceful branch of Anabaptism in the Netherlands led by two brothers, Obbe and Dirk Philips. They rejected the extremes of the Munster group and practiced nonresistance, as did the majority of the Anabaptists. Among this group was a middle-aged man named Menno Simons. Earlier he had begun to study the Scriptures for himself. The Bible study led to his conversion and renunciation of the Catholic Church, in which he was a priest.

Menno Simons was a gifted writer. He wrote about two dozen books and pamphlets which were circulated among the scattered and sometimes confused congregations in the Netherlands. The influence of these writings and his preaching in the churches of this region did much to establish, hold together, strengthen and build up these young congregations.

Soon these scattered groups became known as "Mennists" as a tribute to the leader who had united them. Later they became known as Mennonites, a name that identifies them even today.

BASIC BELIEFS OF THE ANABAPTISTS

What beliefs made the 16th century Anabaptists distinct from other Protestants? What were the points of agreement?

There were two crucial beliefs which Anabaptists held in common with the other Protestant reformers. The first was that the Scriptures are the Word of God and therefore the only basis of authority for the Christian Church. No human tradition or practice can ever be substituted for or added to the Word of God in ordering the life of the Church.

The second common belief was the Anabaptists agreed that salvation cannot be earned by anyone. Salvation and forgiveness of sin are the result of God's grace alone. All people are invited to accept God's saving work in Jesus Christ though faith in him.

No boundaries for the Church

It was in the belief about the nature of the Church, particularly in its relationship to the state, that the Anabaptists disagreed most with the other reformers.

As the Protestant Reformation developed, both Luther and Zwingli faced strong challenges from the political rulers of their time. In certain cases the reformers gave to the political rulers the final decision on which reforms would be made and which would not. The result was the state-church system in which the church and the secular state worked hand in hand. Under this system, those who lived in a given political jurisdiction were considered to be part of the church in that area.

This the Anabaptists could not accept. They believed that *the church was a voluntary community of people who had committed themselves to faithfully follow Jesus Christ.* No political or geographical boundaries could determine the composition of the true church, they maintained. The church and the state must be separate. There were in fact two kingdoms—the kingdom of God and the kingdom of this world. Believers gave themselves to the kingdom of God through the church, whereas the affairs of the kingdom of this world were the concern of those who made no claim to follow Christ.

The Church displays the love of Christ

The Anabaptist interpretation of Romans 12 and 13 was that both the Church and the State are institutions of God. It is the state's function to maintain law and order in a society that is basically non-Christian. In this task the state is required to use law, force, and sometimes violence to restrain an evil person.

In contrast, the church is a fellowship of people who love the Lord and one another. These people refrain from crime and civil disorder not because of the law but because they want to please Christ, to whom they have given themselves in complete obedience. The way of the Church is not force and violence but love—love that is so great that, contrary to human nature, Christians can even love their enemies.

Based on their reading of the Scriptures, the Anabaptists came to the conclusion that *they were called by God to be forgiving, loving followers of Jesus even to the point of suffering for him.* Christians could have no part in the state's function of enforcing the law and controlling evil. In order to follow the letter and spirit of the New Testament, Christians must refrain from participation in the peace-keeping and war-waging of the state. They were to concentrate instead on showing to all people the love of God which had come to them in Christ, particularly within the fellowship of the church.

Against the prevailing view

It was at this particular point that a great difference of under-standing arose between the Anabaptists and the other churches of that day. The Roman Catholic Church believed the pope had two swords: the sword of the spirit (the Word of God) by which he ruled the church, and the sword of steel by which he ruled the kings of the earth. As the pope lost political power through military defeats, this view changed. But the Roman Catholic Church still saw no problem with Christians participating fully in the use of force, even killing those who were considered enemies or evil persons.

The view of Luther was somewhat different. He held that Christians as individuals were obligated to practice the teachings of Jesus, but that when a Christian was serving as a citizen of the state, these principles did not apply in the same way. As a citizen a Christian could legitimately use force, even kill others if they were evil or considered to be enemies of the state. So Luther too believed that there were two kingdoms, each with its own set of principles; however he felt that a Christian could participate in both even when his life as a citizen directly contradicted his life as a Christian.

This view has become the prevailing view in most Protestant churches today. Most Christians feel there is no conflict between being a faithful Christian and being a part of the military enterprise whose primary purpose at any point can become destruction of the enemy that Christ commands us to love.

They took God's Word seriously

At the very center of Anabaptist beliefs was the conviction that *all Christians are called to obey all the teachings and examples of Christ and his apostles in all circumstances of life.* The Ten Commandments and the Sermon on the Mount meant much to them, and they tried hard to avoid "selective obedience" to the Word of God. They called this commitment to complete obedience, discipleship.

This understanding of the Bible meant the Anabaptists took at literal face value the "hard sayings" of Jesus, as they were often called. When Jesus said that his followers should not go to court, this was what he meant, said the Anabaptists. When Jesus told his disciples that they were not to swear because all oaths ultimately led to invoking God's name (Matthew 23:16-22), the Anabaptists took this at face value. Instead of swearing, they simply affirmed their intention to tell the truth at all times.

They took seriously the words of Jesus who taught that treasures should not be stored up on earth but rather invested in God's kingdom (Matthew 6:19). Jesus taught and the early church demonstrated a spirit of sharing wealth with one another and with those in need in a spirit of love (Acts 4:32). All these things the Anabaptist saw as binding for Christians, and they tried to put them into practice in very concrete ways.

Jesus also taught his followers not to resist evildoers (Matthew 5:39), not to take revenge (5:38-42), and to love rather than hate enemies (5:43-44). These teachings too the Anabaptists followed very carefully. They not only refused to fight and defend themselves when attacked; they also refused to retaliate when they were wronged. They practiced turning the other cheek. They refused to bear arms. To be a part of an effort to kill another human being was to them unthinkable in light of Christ's teaching.

In short, the Anabaptists *put Christ and his kingdom first in their lives.* Because the state saw such practices as dangerous, it persecuted people who held such beliefs. For many believers this meant suffering and for some it meant death.

Mervin Dick

Finding Words for Nonresistant Love

In the year 1569 a believer by the name of Dirk Willems from Holland learned that some officers were on their way to his home to arrest him. He ran out the back door to escape, with the officers chasing him. When they came to a frozen dyke, Willems crossed the ice to the other side. But the officer who was chasing him broke through the ice. When Willems saw that the officer was about to drown in the freezing water, he turned around, made his way back across the ice and helped the officer out of the water. How was Dirk Willems rewarded for his act of compassion? He was arrested by the same officer, brought to trial, and sentenced to be burned at the stake as an Anabaptist heretic.

Mennonites, along with the Quakers and the Church of the Brethren, are called "Historic Peace Churches." This means that throughout their histories these Christians have followed the way of peace and nonresistance.

What is meant by "the way of peace"?

To live by the way of peace is to practice love, caring and peaceful relations with other people in all circumstances of life, in war-time as well as in peace-time. Those who live the way of peace do not defend themselves against murder, rape and looting, but instead "turn the other cheek," "go the second mile" in accordance with the teachings of Jesus in the Sermon on the Mount.

The way of peace means to be wronged rather than do wrong. It means to die rather than to kill, even in self-defense or in warfare. It means to follow the way of absolute love, placing ourselves in God's care, willing to suffer if necessary.

Sometimes this way of peace is called nonresistance, meaning that those who practice it are unarmed and offer no resistance to force.

If the Turks should come...

The early Anabaptist leaders who were introduced in the last chapter made statements about the way of peace out of their study of the Bible. Conrad Grebel, who became one of the founders of the Mennonite church, wrote in 1524: "The gospel and its adherents are not to be protected by the sword, nor are they thus to protect themselves....Neither do they use worldly sword or war, since all killing has ceased with them."*

Michael Sattler, who was part of the circle of brothers with Conrad Grebel and Felix Manz in Zurich, wrote the following in 1527 at a time when the great foreign threat was the Turks: "If the Turks should come, we ought not to resist them. For it is written (Matthew 5:21): Thou shalt not kill. We must not defend others of our persecutors, but are to beseech God with earnest prayer to repel and resist them."

Among the early leaders of the Swiss and South German Anabaptists, the most kindly spirit was said to be Hans Denck. It was he who first used the phrase that has become a key saying among Mennonites today: "No one may know Christ except he follow Him in life."

In 1527 Denck wrote: "No Christian who wishes to boast in his

* This and the following quotes from the Anabaptist leaders are quoted in *Anabaptism in Outline,* Walter Klaassen, editor. (Scottdale, PA: Herald Press, 1981).

Lord may use power to coerce and rule. For the realm of our King consists alone in the teaching and power of the spirit. Whoever truly acknowledges Christ as Lord ought to do nothing but what he commands him."

Let God repay evil

In Austria one of the expressions of Anabaptism was a group of people who banded together to live in a communal lifestyle, sharing all their goods as they lived together in colonies. Because one of the their early influential leaders was a man named Jacob Hutter, later followers in this tradition were called Hutterites.

Within this group there were deep convictions about peace and nonresistance. In 1535 Jacob Hutter wrote to a local political leader: "Our manner of life, our customs and conversation, are known everywhere to all. Rather than wrong any man for a single penny, we would suffer the loss of a hundred gulden, and sooner than strike our enemy with the hand, much less with the spear, or sword, or halbert, as the world does, we would die and surrender life. We carry no weapon, neither spear nor gun, as is clear of the open day."

One of Jacob Hutter's successors in the leadership of this group was a man named Peter Riedmann, a fervent missionary. He left one of the clearest statements on the way of peace to be found among the early Anabaptists:

> *Now since Christ, the Prince of Peace, has prepared and won for himself a kingdom, that is a church, through his own blood; in this same kingdom all worldly warfare has an end as was promised aforetime, "Out of Zion shall go forth the law, and the word of the Lord from Jerusalem, and shall judge among the heathen and shall draw many peoples, so that they shall beat their swords into pruning hooks, sickles and scythes, for from thenceforth nation shall not lift up sword against nation, nor shall they learn war any more."*
>
> *Therefore a Christian neither wages war nor wields the worldly sword to practice vengeance, as Paul also exhorts us, saying, "Dear brothers, avenge not yourselves, but rather give place unto*

the wrath of God, for the Lord saith, "Vengeance is mine; I will repay it." Now...since we are Christ's disciples, we must show forth the nature of him who, though he could, indeed, have done so, repaid not evil with evil.

Now, therefore, Christ desires that we should act even as he did, so he commands us, saying, "It hath been said to the men of old, 'an eye for an eye, and a tooth for a tooth,' but I say unto you, that ye resist not evil; but whosoever shall smite thee on the right cheek, turn and offer to him the other also." Here it is clearly to be seen that one ought neither to avenge oneself nor to go to war, but rather offer back to the strikers his cheeks...that is suffer with patience and wait upon God, who is righteous, and who will repay it.

Weapons to destroy the devil

In Strassburg, Austria, one of the leaders of the Anabaptists was a respected engineer by the name of Pilgram Marpeck. He was well educated and an able spokesman for the believers there. He expressed his views in an article titled "Concerning the Love of God in Christ."

"Christ himself," Marpeck wrote, "in his holy Manhood, submitted to every authority in patience, who himself had and has all authority in heaven and on earth. For whoever takes the sword to make decisions about Christ and himself in the semblance of the Word, takes and uses it like Peter, who cut off Malchus' ear, which Christ put back on and healed."

Marpeck concluded: "If someone today takes and uses the sword thus and fights for Christ the same must and will, according to the words of the Lord, perish by the sword."

Menno Simons, the Dutch Anabaptist leader, worked the hardest at wording the way of peace carefully because many Dutch and German believers were being influenced by Christian movements of the day which justified violence.

Simons too spoke about the kind of weapons which Christians must bear. "Our weapons are not weapons with which cities and countries may be destroyed, walls and gates broken down, and human blood shed in torrents like water. But these are weapons with which the spiritual kingdom and the devil is destroyed and the wicked principle in man's soul is broken down, flinty hearts broken, hearts that have never been sprinkled with the heavenly dew of the Holy Word."

Later in his life Simons wrote, "our weapons are not swords and spears, but patience, silence, and hope, and the Word of God. With these we must maintain our heavy warfare and fight our battle."*

While the basic position of the early Anabaptists was that Christians could not participate in the use of the sword, there were a few instances where this was not the prevailing view. The most notable example of an Anabaptist leader who did not strictly prohibit the use of the sword by Christians was Balthasar Hubmaier. He served as a pastor in the small Austrian town of Waldshut. The congregation he led was the first church to join the Anabaptist movement as a whole congregation in 1525.

While Hubmaier did not absolutely prohibit the involvement of believers in the use of the sword, his position was that it must be used with caution and discernment.

Follow in his steps

Nonresistant love as a way of life has been a consistent characteristic of the confessions of faith of the various Mennonite groups throughout their history.

The first confession of faith for the Mennonite Church is called the Schleitheim Confession, from the town of Schleitheim, Switzerland, where Anabaptist leaders gathered in 1527. Their purpose was to discuss disagreements and to find a common agreement on basic beliefs.

The result of this meeting was that the leaders drew up a confession of faith with seven points, written in simple language that all could understand. Its purpose was to unify the scattered groups of believers in common beliefs as well as to inform and persuade

* From *The Complete Works of Menno Simons.* (Scottdale, PA: Herald Press, 1956), pp. 198, 554.

those who might inquire about the Anabaptists and their understanding of the Bible.

One of the seven points deals with the use of the sword, and gives a basic position which has influenced thinking on the way of peace ever since. The Anabaptist leaders worded their statement as follows:

> *The sword is an ordering of God outside the perfection of Christ. It punishes and kills the wicked, and guards and protects the good. In the law the sword is established over the wicked for punishment and for death, and the secular rulers are established to wield the same.*
>
> *Now many, who do not understand Christ's will for us, will ask: whether a Christian may or should use the sword against the wicked for the protection and defense of the good, or for the sake of love.*
>
> *The answer is unanimously revealed: Christ teaches and commands us to learn from Him, for He is meek and lowly of heart and thus we shall find rest for our souls. Now Christ says to the woman who was taken in adultery, not that she should be stoned according to the law of His Father (and yet He says, "what the Father commanded me, that I do") but with mercy and forgiveness and the warning to sin no more, says: "Go sin no more." Exactly thus should we also proceed.*
>
> *He Himself further forbids the violence of the sword when He says: "the princes of this world lord it over them, etc., but among you it shall not be so." Further Paul says, "Whom God has foreknown, the same he has also predestined to be conformed to the image of his Son," etc. Peter also says: "Christ has suffered* [not ruled] *and has left us an example that you should follow after in his steps."**

In all areas of life

Today, each of the three major Mennonite groups has articles in

---

* From *The Schleitheim Confession.* John Howard Yoder, translator and editor. (Scottdale, PA: Herald Press, 1973), pp. 14-15.

its confession of faith or conference resolutions on the Christian approach to peace.

The Mennonite Church, the largest of the Mennonite groups and sometimes called "the Old Mennonites," adopted the following article as part of its confession of faith in 1963:

We believe that it is the will of God for His children to follow Christ's love in all human relationships. Such a life of love excludes retaliation and revenge. God pours His love into the hearts of Christians so that they desire the welfare of all men. The supreme example of nonresistance is the Lord Jesus Himself. The teaching of Jesus not to resist him who is evil requires the renunciation by His disciples of all violence in human relations. Only love must be shown to all men. We believe that this applies to every area of life; to personal injustice, to situations in which people commonly resort to litigation, to industrial strife, and to international tensions and wars. As nonresistant Christians we cannot serve in any office which employs the use of force. Nor can we participate in military service or in military training, or in the voluntary financial support of war. But we must aggressively, at the risk of life itself, do whatever we can for the alleviation of human distress and suffering.

(Matthew 5:38-48; John 18:36; Romans 5:5; 12:18-21; I Corinthians 6:1-8; II Corinthians 10:3, 4; James 2:8; I Peter 2:23; 4:1) •

The General Conference Mennonite Church adopted a rather lengthy statement in 1971, which it later published as a pamphlet entitled *The Way of Peace*. The statement presents both the biblical basis of the peace position and practical applications for the lives of those who are followers of Christ. The following summary statement from this resolution clearly indicates the meaning of peace for members of this Mennonite group:

"The Christian way is the way of peace. In all our relationships—with God, with neighbors, with nations—Christians are called to live the way of peace. The waging of war is the most obvious and tragic violation of God's will for peace. God does not have two standards of morality—one for government and one for Christians. Warfare is a denial of both the reconciling nature of the Christian gospel and of God's purpose for government (Romans 12:4). All war and all that contributes to war is sin."

The current position of the Mennonite Brethren Church is stated in its 1975 confession of faith:

> *We believe that Christians should live by the law of love and practice the forgiveness of enemies as taught and exemplified by the Lord Jesus. The church, as the body of Christ, is a fellowship of redeemed, separated people, controlled by redemptive love. Its evangelistic responsibility is to present Christ, the Prince of Peace, as the answer to human need, enmity and violence. The evil, brutal and inhuman nature of war stands in contradiction to the new nature of the Christian. The Christian seeks to practice Christ's law of love in all relationships, and in all situations, including those involving personal injustice, social upheaval and international tensions. We believe that it is not God's will that Christians take up arms in military service but that, where possible they perform alternative service to reduce strife, alleviate suffering and bear witness to the love of Christ.*
> *(Exodus 20:1-17; Matthew 5:17-28, 38-45; Romans 12:19-21; 13:8-10; 1 Peter 2:19, 23)*

Notice how all of these statements are based on scriptural foundations, particularly the teachings of Jesus. Notice too how the peace position is applied consistently to all the situations and relationships a Christian must face—personal, social, national and international. The Mennonite Brethren statement in particular connects the way of peace with the evangelistic responsibility of the church.

Love without limits

A very clear, concise, contemporary statement on the way of peace is found in a study booklet by John Paul Wenger titled *Because God Loves* (Herald Press, 1976). Here is a superb statement of how

Mennonites understand the Bible's teaching on peace. The author calls the way of peace "love without limits" and goes on to say:

Our world is broken and divided by the sins of hatred, racism, oppression, and war. Jesus came into this world to heal and unite all people in love and peace. This He did not by force of arms, but through a suffering love that was willing to forgive and keep on loving even to the point of death and apparent defeat. When God raised Jesus from death He was saying that the way of suffering love was not the end, but the way to life.

As the followers of Jesus, our love must reach out to everyone, including our personal and national enemies. In this way we show that we are the children of our Father in heaven, who extends His redemptive love to all.

Making peace in the midst of hostility is possible only when we are willing to suffer in our way of love rather than seeking to destroy the enemy. To destroy the enemy would only cut off all possibility of making peace and experiencing oneness in Jesus. Moreover, life is a sacred trust which only God has the right to end.

The followers of Jesus can have no part in the destruction, hatred, and killing of war. We are willing to suffer imprisonment and even death rather than allow any nation to make us participate in the military machine. Instead, we will forgive all wrongs and seek to build wholeness of life for all.

THE MENNONITE BRETHREN PEACE WITNESS

10

Henry J. Schmidt

One Church's Journey in the Way of Peace

The Oklahoma family was shocked to learn of the US entry into World War I in April of 1917. There was to be a draft. The family had three sons draft age. Their grandparents had migrated to the United States to be free of military conscription. Now they faced the issue again. Newton Baker, Secretary of Defense, ordered all conscientious objectors to report to boot camp with the other draftees. He assured them that some arrangements would be worked out for the Mennonite young men. The family struggled with how to respond to the draft as Mennonite Brethren pacifists. One son decided to migrate to Canada to avoid the draft. The two other sons reported to boot camp as ordered. The issue in boot camp immediately became the level of participation in the war training machine. The one son refused to cooperate with the army—he would not salute the flag or officers, he would not wear army uniforms. This son was court marshalled and sent to federal prison in Leavenworth, Kansas. The third son cooperated with the military. Eleven months after the US entry into the war a system of farm furloughing was worked out for Mennonite men. Conscientious objectors were furloughed from the army to work on farms, including farms in their own communities, as long as it was not the family farm. The third son was furloughed to farm work in his home community.

The peace churches eventually found words to describe their understanding of the Bible's peace message. Starting with the Schleitheim Confession of 1527, Anabaptists have worked with the Scriptures and with the situation of their times to include in their confessions of faith articles about the way of peace.

The previous chapter showed how the three largest Mennonite groups now hold statements of faith about peace which look remarkably similar. Yet each group has its own special way of thinking about peace and of acting out its convictions.

The Mennonite Brethren Church, which began in 1860 in southern Russia, is an Anabaptist church which has integrated strands of evangelicalism and pietism over the course of its development. This chapter will examine the approach to peace of this particular church, then will offer glimpses of the actual peace witness of the Mennonite Brethren in North America since 1917.

The Mennonite Brethren have always been "a people of the book." Their primary concern is to understand and obey the Bible. The Mennonite Brethren peace witness is anchored in a biblical commitment to follow Jesus' model of love and peacemaking, to declare the good news of forgiveness in Jesus Christ, and to give qualified allegiance to the state.

The fruit of a relationship with Jesus

The late Mennonite Brethren church leader John A. Toews wrote in 1975:

> *Christ bears the title 'the Prince of Peace' (Isaiah 9:6); the good news is called 'the gospel of peace' (Ephesians 6:15); God's servants are to be messengers of peace (Isaiah 52:7); and the kingdom of God is designated as the kingdom of peace and righteousness (Romans 14:17). According to these passages peacemaking is at the heart of the gospel. It should therefore be an integral part of the Christian message and ministry (Ephesians 2:17), for when a person is reconciled to God through the forgiveness of sin he becomes a peacemaker, radiating the peace with God he has received through faith in Christ.*

The starting point for the Mennonite Brethren peace witness is the life and teaching of Jesus. Jesus told his disciples, "Blessed are the peacemakers for they shall be called the sons of God" (Matthew 5:6). Mennonite Brethren believe that Christians must take seriously the meaning of Jesus' teaching that "as the father has sent me, even so send I you" (John 17:18). Therefore, Christians must obey Jesus' word about limitless love and forgiveness.

This starting point has three consequences. First, it means that limitless love and nonresistance are the fruit of a personal relationship with Jesus Christ. That makes the Mennonite Brethren peace witness radically different from humanistic pacifism. Jesus as the foundation and model of limitless love raises the discussion of war above the level of escaping military pressures or of killing out of national self-interest. The issue is one of faithfulness and obedience to the lordship of Jesus Christ.

Second, this starting point asks for an application of limitless love in all areas of life—not just in wartime. Christ's example and teaching are the basis for a new way of living. To follow Jesus means to live out his teaching in our homes, schools, churches, labor relations, race relations, professional relations and state relations. Wherever there is enmity or hatred, there Christians show love by word and deed.

Third, it provides Christians with a positive, active strategy for changing society. "Nonresistance" and "conscientious objection" are really not adequate descriptions of the thrust of the Bible, because they fail to capture the active nature of love as the new kingdom weapon. The term "active compassion" better suits the self-giving nature of Christ's love and the love he asks his followers to show.

The church models kingdom values

Mennonite Brethren understand Jesus' call to limitless love as a call to the whole church. They see the church as a fellowship of redeemed and separated people who visibly demonstrate redemptive love. They share the Anabaptist view that the church and state are separate realms which carry out different functions with different standards.

Simply put, the church's main task is to live the values of God's kingdom and to invite others to join that kingdom. Central to kingdom living is a unique way of dealing with evil—suffering the consequences of evil rather than preventing it through force. The world, on the other hand, operates out of the nature of its "prince": with violence, hatred, fear, ill will, intimidation, war and bloodshed.

If the church is to display the reality of Christ's kingdom on earth by living his love ethic, this has an important impact on evangelism. Christians cannot participate in wars and take the lives of people who worship and follow Christ, or of others for whom he died.

Limits of the state

The third factor which has shaped the Mennonite Brethren peace witness is its understanding of the state. It can be summarized in two basic statements. First, the state was instituted by God but holds limited authority over the church. When the claims of government conflict with the claims of God "we must obey God rather than men."

Second, the Christian is called to be a responsible citizen in society. Paul reminds Christians to render to Caesar customs, taxes and honor. To honor those in authority means to take them seriously as the ministers of God. Mennonite Brethren confessions consistently have urged church members to pray for political leaders, to pay their taxes and "to promote justice, respect for human dignity and conditions of peace."

More recently Mennonite Brethren have been urged to remind government leaders of biblical standards concerning morality in matters of justice, war, divorce, abortion, corruption and discrimination.

THE PEACE WITNESS IN NORTH AMERICA

Mennonite Brethren together with other Mennonites first came to North America in 1874. They left Russia when the Russian government withdrew the privileges of religious freedom, military exemption, self-administered German schools, and the village system of life which the Mennonite colonies had enjoyed for a century.

In North America the initial Mennonite Brethren immigrants duplicated their colony lifestyle, settling in small, rural communities that were separated from the world. Their thinking was characterized by an isolationist and survival mindset, and their peace witness was limited primarily to defining the role of the church in a new political environment.

Already in 1878 at their first unofficial convention in Henderson, Nebraska, Mennonite Brethren passed a resolution "that our members are not permitted to hold government office or take part at the polls." In 1890 they agreed to let members "vote quietly in elections," but asked them to refrain from participation and involvement in the conventions of political parties.

Requests for military exemption

The North American entry into World War I came as a shock to the isolated Mennonite Brethren communities. After forty years of peace they were suddenly conscripted into the war efforts of Canada and the U.S. Along with conscription came an American hatred for pacifists and for German culture. Once again Mennonites were forced to decide whether to negotiate for exemption or consider emigration. They chose to appeal to their governments for legislative privileges.

In 1917 a U.S. Mennonite committee with Mennonite Brethren representation traveled to Washington to request military exemption. Mennonite Brethren, together with other representatives from the Mennonites, Friends and Brethren, drafted a plan of action for alternative service again in 1940. In Canada, the government met with three Mennonite representatives in 1940 to negotiate alternatives to military service.

Because of the persistence of the peace group delegation, the Canadian government eventually accepted an alternative service program. And in the U.S., a bill passed in September 1940 opened the way for the Civilian Public Service program under the church's supervision.

Attempts to build credibility

Mennonites of all stripes banded together in 1920 to form the Mennonite Central Committee (MCC). The occasion was the civil war and famine in Russia. A part of the incentive, however, was the need for Mennonites to build credibility in an American environment hostile to their pacifist position. What they needed, wrote P.C. Hiebert, "was an opportunity to disprove the charges of cowardice and selfishness made against the conscientious objector, and to express in a positive, concrete way the principle of peace and good will in which they believed."

Thousands of lives were spared as a result of the Mennonite rehabilitation and relief work in Russia. At the same time, Canadian Mennonites appealed to their government to relax a restrictive immigration law. The law was repealed in 1922. The Canadian Mennonite Board of Colonization resettled some 18,000 Russian Mennonites in Canada during the 1920s.

Mennonite Brethren passed a resolution in 1919 condemning war. But in general, Mennonite Brethren protests to the two wars were cautious, partly because they were suspected of having German sympathies as a German-speaking immigrant group. Official conference resolutions and periodicals expressed strong appreciation for and loyalty to the government during and between the wars.

Most Mennonite Brethren men remained firmly committed to nonresistance during World War I. The response to World War II, however, was not uniform. Melvin Gingerich reports in *Service for Peace* that in the U.S. 39 percent served in alternative service, 34 percent registered as regular combatants, and 26 percent worked as non combatants.

Intensified Bible teaching

World War I and the struggle to gain legal status for conscientious objectors prompted the Mennonite Brethren to reaffirm their historic position against war and military service, and to elect a Committee on Nonresistance in 1919. During the inter-war years the committee was responsible for government negotiations and biblical teaching. An annual Peace Sunday was introduced for the fall.

Many articles on the peace witness were published in Conference periodicals just after World War I and again just prior to World War II. Recurring themes in these writings were the biblical basis of nonresistance, the sinful nature of war, the warning that war was imminent, and the appeal to follow Jesus by choosing alternative service.

Through this process Mennonite Brethren began to distinguish between biblical nonresistance and the humanistic pacifist movement of the inter-war years. Mennonite Brethren strongly emphasized nonresistance as the lifestyle of the Christian, not simply a stance for war. They also saw that pacifism was empty without a personal commitment to Jesus Christ.

The commitment of Mennonite Brethren to proclaim the gospel has always taken precedence over other attempts to transform society. In 1924 they agreed that "our greatest mission consists in proclaiming the gospel of salvation, which leads to the renewing of the inner man, for without regeneration no true or lasting peace can be attained."

Mission and service

Mission and service belong together in the Anabaptist vision. The Mennonite Brethren peace witness has had a strong humanitarian dimension. Through the denominational Board of General Welfare and Mennonite Central Committee, Mennonite famine victims in Russia and Mennonite immigrants from Russia to Canada and South America received massive assistance of food, clothing, jobs, agricultural equipment, money to purchase land and to pay travel debts. At first the recipients of this good will were primarily other Mennonites, but after World War II the focus broadened.

Also after World War II, Mennonite Brethren moved into missions more aggressively than at any time in their history. In the 15 years following the war recruits for missions, MCC and Christian service as well as giving to missions and relief increased 100 percent. By 1960 the mission church population outnumbered North American members by 32,700 to 29,200.

The mission thrust was a positive strategy for changing the world in which Mennonite Brethren assumed that man's alienation from God can be resolved only by reconciliation through Christ. They placed primacy on gospel proclamation rather than on political and social change. And yet this expanded mission thrust was accompanied by a growing social conscience. The four-point program outlined by the Board of Missions included evangelism, church building, education and medical work.

Broadening application of nonresistance

As more and more North American Mennonite Brethren moved from rural to urban settings during the post-war years, they were forced to clarify and broaden their nonresistant position. A laxness in teaching nonresistance had crept into the church, as a 1948 denominational statement acknowledged:

> *The Committee of Reference and Counsel deeply regrets that we have brethren in our churches who do not live according to the teaching of Jesus and the Apostles in their personal lives but in times of war desire to be nonresistant. Such inconsistent Christian living darkens our testimony before the world and causes young people to look upon the principle of nonresistance which we confess in our churches, negatively and with disdain.*

Several surveys from the 1950s indicate that many churches gave little attention to the teaching of nonresistance. In view of this, the church tried to reorientate a new generation in a stronger, more theologically-developed, nonresistance position. This education was done primarily through sermons, peace study conferences, conference resolutions and church publications.

A second factor which forced Mennonite Brethren to rework their position was new church/state issues which called for a broader application of nonresistant principles in society—among them law suits, labor-management conflicts, peacetime conscription, civil defense, payment of taxes and racism. In 1957 Mennonite Brethren resolved to apply nonresistance beyond war. "We believe and teach," they agreed, "that it applies to every phase of life, to all relationships, personal, social, economic, political, national and international."

One new challenge which urban Mennonite Brethren faced was to live out their nonresistance in the arena of labor conflicts and union membership. As early as 1955 various voices within the church discouraged participation in labor unions. Mennonite Brethren agreed with organized labor on the concern for worker welfare and on "collective bargaining" as a means of improving worker conditions, but they disliked the strikes, violence and large-scale protests associated with the unions.

Politics as a new mission field

The 1960s and 1970s signaled a new era in the Mennonite Brethren peace witness. The church changed significantly in its view on participation in government. By 1980, for example, Mennonite Brethren had an acting governor of South Dakota, three federal legislators in Ottawa, one Canadian cabinet minister, and numerous state and provincial political candidates and elected representatives. Through MCC they had paid information monitors in Washington and Ottawa.

Both in 1966 and 1978 General Conference statements assumed greater involvement in social and political affairs. Missions became the reason for increased involvement. "The Christian church has been given a mandate to bring Christian concerns to bear in all situations," Mennonite Brethren agreed in 1978. "We have been instructed to bring the gospel to 'all the world' (Mark 16:15) and that directive allows for no exception in terms of either geography or society."

Challenged to live out limitless love

In recent years the growing complexity of church/state relations has called Mennonite Brethren to state their peace witness even more clearly. Mennonite Brethren peace statements in the past two decades reflect two trends. The first is a concern to give a more thorough biblical, theological and practical rationale for the peace position.

The second trend is the shift from the term "nonresistance" to the term "limitless love." Canadian churchman John Redekop called members in 1973 to reconnect Christian nonresistance with its source— the central Christian doctrine of love. "Having failed largely to root nonresistance in Christian love," he suggested, "the major emphasis has gradually shifted to avoidance, although a moment's reflection reminds us that the entire thrust of love, especially Christian love, is exactly the opposite."

While this rediscovered emphasis on "limitless love" has broadened the scope and application of the peace witness to an ever-widening circle of relationships in everyday life, Mennonite Brethren have not always been able to agree on how love was to be expressed. For example, a 1972 study of Mennonite Brethren by Kauffman and Harder revealed that 83 percent of Mennonite Brethren felt that capital punishment should be retained.

Reaffirm peace witness for the 1980s

The US and Canadian Conferences as well as the General Conference have reaffirmed the peace witness for the 1980s. The US Conference in 1980 "affirmed our Mennonite Brethren Confession of Faith and historic peace position," and called for more systematic Bible teaching regarding peacemaking. The General Conference in 1981 also reaffirmed the Confession of Faith and expressed concern about churches and pastors who view the peace teaching as optional. "This we consider to be a serious violation of our peace position and the teachings of Jesus," the Conference asserted. In 1984 the Canadian Conference not only made a similar statment but also went on record to support participation in peace marches when such participation is carefully processed with the local church. The same Conference also spoke out against nuclear war while calling for a more public peace witness and more teaching on peace issues in the churches.

NUCLEAR BOMB AND
LIBERATION BULLET

11

Howard J. Loewen

How Do They Rate Against the Just War Theory

For many years Billy Graham has preached about peace with God to large audiences around the world. In 1978 he began to speak out about the global arms race, and in particular about nuclear weapons. "The nuclear issue is not just a political issue," he said at the time. "It is a moral and spiritual issue as well." Graham said he was not a pacifist and did not favor unilateral disarmament, but said he could see no way "in which nuclear war could be branded as being God's will. Such warfare, if it ever happens, will come because of the greed and pride of the human heart." When asked why he had changed his thinking on this question, Graham replied, "I have gone back to the Bible to restudy what it says about the responsibilities we have as peacemakers. I have seen that we must seek the good of the whole human race, and not just the good of any one nation."

Throughout history one of the church's main positions on war has been the just war theory (JWT). This view states that war is acceptable under certain conditions. Today people are showing a renewed interest in the JWT. Some are reacting strongly against this view, while others are finding new ways to apply it.

Two vivid events, etched into the memory of the twentieth-century mind, form the backdrop for the modern church's thinking about war. One is Hiroshima and the other is Vietnam.

The bombing of Hiroshima triggered the nuclear age. The United States won an armed conflict with nuclear might. Now the world would have to live under the threat of the bomb.

The American defeat in Vietnam symbolized the effectiveness of the liberation revolution. The U.S. lost "a war of liberation." Now the world would have to live under the threat of the liberation bullet.

These two threats are related. The nuclear build-up of the northern hemisphere is, to a large extent, being done at the political, social and economic expense of the southern hemisphere. The violence that is waged against the south in order to maintain the goals of the north is greater than the south can bear. The seeds for revolution are being sown in many places.

How can we discuss the just war theory meaningfully today? One way is to discuss it with the nuclear bomb and the liberation bullet in mind. Let's try it.

The history of the just war theory

The JWT was born in the third century following a long period of early church pacifism. Constantine had just conquered the entire Roman Empire, and made Christianity the faith of the empire. Against this background the church father Augustine developed a doctrine of just war which could be applied to pagan people and Christian heretics alike. Under certain conditions Christians could fight to protect the interests of the state and the church.

During the medieval period Thomas Aquinas was the foremost proponent of the JWT. He made one major addition to Augustine's just war doctrine: he allowed the violent overthrow of an unjust government. However, the JWT seriously declined during this period as a means of dealing with wars and conflicts, and the just war code was frequently violated.

The churches of the Protestant Reformation went beyond the medieval JWT in the direction of making war more acceptable. Luther and Lutheranism taught that the citizen has a duty to obey the state. This allowed the state to step up its preparations for war.

Calvin and Calvinism also strongly endorsed JWT. However, the Reformed churches moved more in the direction of the crusade, partly because they thought of the church as a holy nation.

Both Lutheran and Reformed contributions strengthened the power of the state and made war more acceptable. This led to a century of religious warfare and intolerance.

After many decades of religious wars there was a marked change in mood brought about by the Enlightenment. The peace themes of earlier times were revived. The JWT was re-examined within the environment of growing pacifism and secularism. But the wars of nationalism in the nineteenth century ended that optimism and began to usher in a new period of world history.

Our contemporary church and world have witnessed a significant revival of the JWT. World War II brought in the age of Auschwitz and Hiroshima and forced people to consider old questions about war. The atrocities at Auschwitz seemed to justify war; the atrocities at Hiroshima seemed to outlaw war.

The just war doctrine also emerged clearly as a powerful force in the conscience of America during the Vietnam War. It served as a test-case for the rules of war.

The rules of war

An official list of the right conditions and conduct for a just war do not exist. There are no official documents that spell out the criteria clearly and completely, even though after the Reformation this doctrine became part of what it meant to be a confessing Christian. However, the JWT can be outlined in the following way.

Eight criteria provide the basis for determining a just war. The first four deal with the just conditions for war—the bases on which war can be justified.

Just intention requires the right attitude which does not harbor revenge or anger. It also involves the restoration of peace, granting mercy and not vengeance to the defeated, not requiring unconditional surrender, and the restoration of justice. The underlying intention must be peacemaking.

Just authority deals with the decision-making process. A lawful, legitimate authority must declare war. The highest governmental authority must sanction it. *Just cause* means that there must be a clear offense that is worthy of response.

Last resort insists that only when negotiation, mediation, and compromise have failed can a nation engage in armed conflict.

The second four criteria deal with just conduct in war. *Reasonable hope of success* means that war is conducted by military methods which promise reasonable hope of winning the war. It is not sufficient simply to have a just cause.

Limited ends involves a definite relationship between the methods one uses and the ends one is trying to accomplish in a war. An entire city should not be destroyed to capture a small group of enemy soldiers. Unconditional surrender, excessive force, or utter destruction of a nation are questionable. Human nature is to be respected.

Proportionate means refers to the reasonable expectation that the good result of the war will exceed the horrible evils it brings. This applies to war in general and to tactics in particular.

Finally, *non-combatant immunity* requires that civilians not involved in the manufacture, direction, or use of arms must not be attacked. Non-combatant casualties are permissible if they are not intended. If large numbers of non-combatants, prisoners-of-war, injured, and/or civilians are affected, the principle of proportionality is violated.

THE THREAT OF NUCLEAR WAR

What happens when the rules of the JWT are applied to nuclear and counter-revolutionary wars?

Most people respond to the possibility of nuclear war in one of four basic ways. Let's evaluate each approach against the rules of the just war.

Unlimited nuclear war

One group of people would be willing to fight an unlimited nuclear war if provoked. The basic policies of the USA and the USSR are to retaliate in kind if one attacks the other—to the point of virtual annihilation. This is a policy of mutually assured destruction.

In the event of a USSR massive first strike on the USA the JWT criteria could never be met. Just intention, just cause, prior declaration of war, reasonable hope of success (not just winning but preserving), limited ends or moderation, non-combatant immunity, and proportionality are all not possible because both sides would be completely destroyed.

Limited nuclear war

Other people propose three more limited kinds of nuclear war.

(1) The *strategic nuclear war* involves the direct targeting of population centers such as large cities. However, this violates the JWT's demand for protection of non-combatants. The direction of recent American nuclear policy, the destructive trading of cities planned during the Cuban missile crisis in 1962, and the obliteration bombing of World War II that destroyed whole cities suggest that the U.S. is open to considering such a war.

(2) The *tactical nuclear war* involves limited nuclear attack on military targets. This limited strategy is now becoming an official part of USA and USSR nuclear policy. This has created a belief in the possibility of nuclear war by suggesting that limited nuclear warfare is less horrible than an all-out nuclear war.

Church leaders and theologians are divided on their response to the idea of nuclear war. Some argue that limited nuclear attacks against specific military targets can be justified on the basis of the JWT. The large number of non-combatants that would be killed—thus violating the criterion of non-combatant immunity—is justified on the grounds that their death was not intended.

The case against this position is illustrated by the response of the Catholic bishops of America in 1983. They reject this position because of the danger of fallout on population areas and because of the possibility of escalation once the leap from conventional to nuclear weapons has been made.

(3) The *deterrence without use* involves having enough nuclear

weapons so that they serve as a threat. This policy states that it is not wrong to build and stockpile nuclear weapons even though it is wrong to use them. Their only purpose is to deter enemy nations from starting anything. Until recently this was the official USA policy.

Some people argue that since World War II deterrence has worked and is the basis for stability. The question is how long can you keep it secret that you have no intention of actually using nuclear weapons? This position lacks credibility.

The result of this approach, however, is to justify the current policy of nuclear stockpiling, thereby increasing the risk of accidental nuclear war. This policy therefore only makes the problem worse with no change in sight.

Nuclear pacifism

There is a growing number of people who, on the basis of the JWT, are concluding that the only viable position in our time is nuclear pacifism. These people are using JWT to reject nuclear warfare.

The age of Hiroshima and Vietnam has produced a major shift in this generation's sense of the rightness of modern warfare. Many people are now calling for bilateral, and even unilateral, nuclear disarmament between the superpowers. Although these people are willing, on the basis of the JWT, to acknowledge the need for non-nuclear forms of defense and war, they use the moral rules of the JWT to outlaw the production, deployment and use of nuclear weapons under any conditions.

Total pacifism

Some people want to abandon weapons altogether, even though they are very conscious that war and the making of war will always be with the human family. There are different types of pacifism emerging from varying philosophies. However, they all reject the JWT as the way in which the church and society should respond to war.

This does not mean that some do not see value in using JWT as a basis to respond to war. An increasing number of pacifists encourage a more rigorous application of the JWT. But they see it as a secondary and not primary answer to the question of war.

The rules for just war seriously challenge those who advocate nuclear warfare.

WARS OF LIBERATION

Beyond the nuclear threat we must also apply the JWT criteria to wars of liberation. The struggle for justice is a crucial issue in our time. Violence in our day is much more widespread than we like to admit. It is present not only in obvious acts of war, but also in more subtle forms that characterize the structures of our society.

The victims of this "structural violence" are a majority of the human family. They suffer from political, economic, social and spiritual oppression. Those who enjoy the advantages of the present structures of our society are a minority of the human family, yet they possess the most power.

Can the change from an unjust to a just situation come about peacefully? Can those with power be persuaded to give any of that power to the powerless? Or must the powerless use violence to bring about justice?

The problem of unjust structures has led some to argue that there is a stronger justification for revolution than for most traditional wars. These people have dusted off the doctrine of the just revolution to support their argument. Where did this doctrine start?

"Just revolution"

In the twelfth century an English pastor, John of Salisbury, wrote that when the prince disobeys the law he becomes a tyrant, and that it is just for public tyrants to be killed and the people set free for the service of God. In the thirteenth century Thomas Aquinas, in a more moderate way, came close to defining a doctrine of just revolution against unjust governments.

Martin Luther in the sixteenth century hinted at a doctrine of just revolution when a combination of emperor and pope faced off against the Protestant princes. He wrote that the princes must resist the tyrants. His basic position, however, was that rebellion against lawful authority is unjust.

A few years later, Thomas Muentzer used Luther's teachings to support rebellion in a way that Luther never dreamed of. He led a peasant revolt against the authorities of his day.

John Calvin called for strong authority in government, and at the same time he authorized magistrates to oppose tyrants who betrayed the freedom of the people. Later Calvinism became a revolutionary force in several societies. For example, Beza, Calvin's successor, endorsed resistance to tyrants. Likewise the English Puritans frequently became revolutionaries.

Thus, within the just war tradition a doctrine of just revolution was formulated. Can this doctrine be used to justify the liberation wars throughout the world today?

Applying the just war code

Is it ever right for the Christian to use violence to overthrow an oppressive government? To answer that question, let's apply the traditional criteria of the JWT to "just revolution."

The requirement of *just intention* is one of the most difficult to meet. The origin of revolution usually arises out of a deep sense of anger at injustices. During early stages of a revolution the personal risk is high. But after the revolutionaries have tasted success this rule must be rigorously applied, for revolutions can easily degenerate into one tyranny replacing another tyranny.

The criterion of *just authority* is the most difficult to apply. The revolutionaries find it difficult to establish themselves as just authorities. But it should be remembered that a justly elected government that has strayed from its moral and legal obligation is also unable to establish its own legitimacy. Many revolutionaries, therefore, use Jesus and the Bible as the legitimate authority to warrant revolution in an oppressive situation.

The importance of *just cause* is perhaps more easily applied. It calls for a clear offence. The structural violence experienced by many people under oppressive governments provides the evidence they need.

The criterion of *last resort* has a wide range of responses. A government in power will always believe that a revolution is premature, while the revolutionaries will insist that they should have revolted long before the actual outburst took place.

All violence looks the same

The *reasonable chance of success* of a revolution is dicey at best. Classical JWT says it is wrong to engage others in a lost cause. If the revolution fails, the repressive regime will likely become more repressive. To be responsible, revolutionaries must carefully count the cost ahead of time.

Many revolutionaries re-interpret the JWT at this point. They argue that the most important objective of revolutionary movements is not to win victories but to stay in existence as a continuing threat until the unjust government is overthrown. Thus, the criterion of success can be met, they contend.

The criterion of *limited ends* is just as difficult to insure in the process of fighting as it is to measure success in advance of it. Very quickly the violence of the oppressed becomes indistinguishable from the violence of the oppressor.

Likewise the criterion of *proportionate means* raises the question of how much violence can now be justified in the hope of avoiding more extended violence later. How does a fighter keep raw anger in check? The very nature of modern guerrilla warfare, which is not limited to military targets, makes it extremely difficult to control the extent of violence.

Finally, the requirement of *non-combatant immunity* is not met by revolution. Guerrilla warfare, in its attempt to overcome oppressive governments, must use tactics that destroy villages and civilians. It simply cannot limit its destruction to military targets. Innocent people get killed regularly and indiscriminately.

This completes our exploration of how the the dual threats of nuclear and revolutionary wars look when we apply the just war code to them. We have found that both situations are seriously jeopardized by the JWT. We have also seen the workability and relevance of the JWT cast in doubt by these modern wars.

In the next chapter we will go on to carefully assess whether the just war theory itself is an adequate way for the Christian to respond to war in the modern world.

Howard J. Loewen

Does the Theory Match the Bible's Vision?

During World War II the US Navy desperately needed chaplains. Hence someone suggested that they recruit men directly from theological seminaries and put them into the chaplaincy without any previous pastoral experience. It was a mistake they never repeated. But I was one of the forty they recruited.

Within a week after graduation I was in the Navy. And in a few months I was in the South Pacific, assigned to the First Marine Division. Being in a war posed no theological problems for me. Reformed theology had long since eased my conscience with its "just war theory." I felt that my participation with the marines— trained for assault operations— was pleasing to God. I carried no weapon, so would not personally do the enemy any harm. Besides, I was an evangelical, and those marines needed the gospel of Jesus Christ. My burden was the possibility of their dying without the knowledge of his salvation.

Our first operation was against a Japanese stronghold (Cape Gloucester, New Britain). On Christmas Eve (1943) I gathered with quite a few Marines on the deck of our LST. The assault was scheduled before dawn the next day. We sang some carols. I read the Christmas story, spoke of God's condescension, and we prayed. All were inwardly "ruminating the morrow's danger." So far as the Marines were concerned it was to be "Merry Christmas to the Nips!"

A day or so later I was advancing along with some others over the area that had been hotly contested. It was raining. I recall the mud, the debris on the battlefield and the stench of human flesh rotting in the tropical heat. Then to my right I saw what had been an enemy strongpoint. The treadmarks of one of our tanks went right over it. It had been crushed and some bodies were scattered about.

My attention was particularly drawn to what had been a Japanese soldier, lying in the mud. His head was missing. The sight was altogether revolting. I turned aside, but then found myself almost unconsciously drawn back to him. For what caught my attention, and what piqued my curiosity was a little book half buried in the mud alongside where his head should have been. I had to see what that book was. I can still recall the revulsion and the smell as I forced myself to reach down and grasp the book.

You guessed! It was a Japanese New Testament. Had this horrible refuse been my brother? I was greatly troubled. A verse of Scripture came to mind: Galatians 6.10, "As we have opportunity, let us do good to all men, and especially to those who are of the household of faith." What was I, a Christian, doing there at Cape Gloucester? Somehow, the "just war theory" on that day and in that place seemed like so much unwarranted nonsense. And you can be sure that I've not been the same since! (Arthur Glasser, Professor of Missions, Fuller School of World Mission, June 25, 1985).

In chapter 11 we measured two war realities of our time against the just war theory (JWT). In this chapter we will turn the tables slightly and judge the JWT by its applicability and by the vision of the Bible.

The JWT does have moral value. Its intention is to limit violence, even though there is little evidence of its effectiveness. In the history of the church the JWT has usually functioned to justify war rather than to judge it.

Yet it is better to have some kind of restraint on the conditions and means of war than none at all. In a world that will always be riveted with violence and war it is still possible to hope that the JWT could be used to steer the church and society toward more peace. That is one of the challenges today for Christians who hold this view.

Perhaps the present dangers of nuclear and revolutionary wars can help the JWT become an ethical instrument to reject rather than justify war. Could it direct people toward a biblical perspective that judges all wars in a nuclear age to be wrong? A consistent application of the JWT criteria today renders both nuclear and revolutionary wars unjustifiable—more clearly so than with regard to other kinds of war in history.

Above all, the church and society must be strongly encouraged actually to *use* the JWT. Perhaps this would lead the church back once again to the prophetic position of the early church regarding war and peace—namely, a biblical pacifism.

Yet on the whole the JWT has not and does not sufficiently represent a thorough-going Christian ethic. The following criticisms demonstrate its serious inadequacy as the ground for Christian actions and attitudes toward war and peace in our day.

INADEQUATE FOR THE THE REALITIES OF WAR

Mass destruction

The horror of modern warfare makes JWT ineffective. Although JWT condemns any use of weapons of mass destruction, it breaks down completely when weapons are designed to destroy nameless civilians indiscriminately. Therefore, the technology of modern warfare alone puts the JWT out of date.

Similarly, the technology and tactics of modern guerrilla warfare make the criteria of JWT virtually impossible to apply. The widespread and massive destruction of such warfare, and the even more serious destruction of the established authorities seeking to squelch revolutions, violates every rule of the JWT.

International Christians

Christians should not and cannot be involved in killing other Christians. Christians are one in the body of Christ. The long history of warfare in the "christianized" west has repeatedly violated this fundamental truth. Christians have repeatedly killed each other.

Now, in the nuclear age, this killing can be increased in geometric proportions. If then we apply the JWT rules we would have to condemn all wars in which Christians participated—past, present and future. In the same way, revolutionary warfare increases many times over the reality of Christians killing Christians.

Official condemnation

Never has a body of bishops or a major denominational body officially condemned a war. Since its beginning in the fourth century the JWT has remained a theory. It has never really worked. The implementation of the JWT criteria represents a history of failure.

However, there are some signs today that official religious bodies and leaders are willing to take positions against the nuclear threat based on the JWT. Unfortunately, this emerging pacifism is frequently cancelled out by a corresponding willingness on the part of northern hemisphere Christians to support and justify counter-revolutionary violence in the southern hemisphere in the name of justice.

Moral function

The JWT has seldom been used as a tool for moral guidance. Until recent times, proponents of the JWT usually have been able to justify the wars of their own nations. The theory was originally formulated to show that some wars might be an exception to the gospel, yet it has become a tool to justify every war that comes along.

In addition, nations serve as judges in their own cases during the threat of war. Therefore, who is to say that all alternatives have been exhausted? The JWT implies that there will be truthful presentation of all the facts by a nation to its people before and during war, allowing Christians to make informed judgments. However, this has never happened.

Finally, the JWT simply has too many loopholes. Proponents can find ways to justify any war. For the appeal of the JWT to be credible, its criteria must be stated more clearly and firmly, and its effectiveness demonstrated in actually limiting war.

Self-righteous justification

The JWT assumes that one side will be just and the other unjust. Yet in times of war, without exception, both sides claim their cause to be just. Perhaps we should conclude from this that no nation can be just. There is much that is unjust on both sides.

The injustice on both sides is only heightened when today there are two super-powers each sufficiently armed to annihilate human civilization. Each has self-righteously driven the other to the point of mutually assured destruction.

Fusing church and society

The JWT was born in a church established and supported by the Roman Empire under the emperor Constantine. It therefore has a conservative bias regarding the relation of the church to the state. Its vision of church-state relations is one which links together the church and society in such a way that the church is supportive of the state.

In this environment the church can justify the use of force to bring about its desired ends for society. It comes to see war as a police function which maintains peace and order and resists violence and tyranny.

The JWT continues to function with this understanding of the Constantinian vision. This is true whether it is the church in the northern hemisphere joined to a capitalist society which can justify nuclear war, or whether it is the church in the southern hemisphere joined to a Marxist movement which can justify revolutionary wars in the name of Christ.

Both the classical just war and the contemporary just revolution waged in the name of Christ exemplify the Constantinian orientation of the JWT which fuses church and society as ethical agents of change in a questionable way.

Natural law tradition

The JWT is too extensively grounded in the natural law tradition of the Greeks and Romans. Reliance on natural law means that you appeal to that point of view in society which makes the most political sense. That is true whether one lives in a Constantinian, capitalist or communist society.

To be politically realistic, people appeal to that which makes the most sense in the context of a given society. Therefore Christians—whether in ancient or modern society—have justified war in terms of defending the world and culture in which they lived because that made the most sense to them and they had the most to gain from it.

The origins of the JWT in this natural law tradition have provided the basis for the Christian church invariably and uncritically to support wars fought by nation states or national movements.

This kind of strong reliance on national politics has overshadowed the primary source of authority to which Christians and the church claim to appeal in judging questions of war and peace—namely, biblical revelation.

Must not the origin of the Christian position on war come from the Bible? Does not the teaching of Scripture, and that of Jesus Christ in particular, clearly challenge the very basis on which the JWT is built? Is not the biblical vision of peace and the early church's witness to peace a sign of the true biblical and theological position for our age?

These questions focus the most fundamental criticism against the JWT—that it is not sufficiently biblical and theological in its orientation.

FALLS SHORT OF THE BIBLE

The assumptions of the JWT are not rooted deeply enough in the biblical vision of the gospel of peace and salvation. Therefore the moral power of the JWT has eroded during the present time. The Christian politics of medieval Europe and modern America, which have nurtured this tradition, have essentially collapsed. As a result the JWT increasingly has become an inadequate moral instrument to deal with the most profound ethical issue of our nuclear age.

The sinfulness of human nature

One of the major weaknesses of the JWT is its understanding of human nature. On the one hand, it tends to use the argument of the fallenness of human nature to justify the use of force to contain violence. On the other hand, it appeals to enlightened human reason in applying the criteria of the JWT so that fighting a just war is possible.

What is not sufficiently clear in the JWT is that warfare has its roots in the fallness of human nature, and that war itself is the climax of rebellion against God and humanity. In the Bible sin as disobedience, violence as an outcome of deep insecurity, and warfare as an expression of human hatred are very closely related. The rapid escalation of violence from Adam to Cain to Lamech to Noah to Nimrod in Genesis supplies convincing evidence of this sinfulness.

Today the murder of Abel by Cain has the possibility of being magnified to include the entire human race. The JWT does not sufficiently contribute to the recognition that modern societies have produced a nuclear Cain. Nuclear weapons provide a devastatingly clear picture of human cursing and murdering. The human heart, not God, is the root of all destruction. The inner attitude of collective hatred has led to the self-righteous building of murderous weapons that can annihilate an entire population of Abels.

The sovereignty of God, the warrior

The JWT does not sufficiently affirm that God has entered the arena of human conflict as a warrior to eliminate violence rather than justify it. God has chosen to participate in the sinful history of humanity in order to defeat the evil forces contributing to violence, injustice and chaos. The holy wars of God recorded in the Bible are fought toward this end. Thus God fights both for and against Israel. Here the sovereignty and lordship of God the warrior are demonstrated. The focus is on *his* involvement and control in war rather than on human involvement and control.

God's wars in biblical history are ultimately fought by the Word of God, by miracle, and by faith, not with sword and armies under human control. When Israel begins to replace her dependence on God as warrior with an idolatrous dependence on the nation and the king as warrior, she comes under the judgment of God, and the Lord fights—that is, brings judgment—against her.

The JWT does not sufficiently recognize the idolatry of national sovereignty. The nation state has become one of the main gods of our civilization. There exists a tendency, deeply rooted in our culture, to preserve that god at any cost. The JWT frequently has contributed to this idol worship.

The idolization of the nation state and the bomb increasingly propel us toward self-destruction. The JWT does not have a sufficiently realistic grasp of the fact that the nation state is an agent of the principalities and powers of this world. Modern rebellious and idolatrous states are now willing to sacrifice any number of human beings on the altar of the god of national sovereignty.

If the false god is not clearly identified in the assumptions of the JWT, neither is the nature and way of the true God. Accordingly, in the JWT the reality of God's judgment regarding the warring ways of the nations is severely minimized. What the JWT does not recognize is that God's judgment is a far more awesome threat than the menace of a nuclear enemy or a revolutionary movement.

The illusions by which nation states live are foolishness in God's eyes. The JWT does not bring this perspective to bear on today's nuclear situation. Instead it has contributed to the development of the bomb which reflects the colossal self-righteousness of nuclear nations.

From the perspective of the biblical vision, the judgment of God lies in allowing these nations to head toward self-destruction. As in the days of Noah, God may choose to let this rebellion be limitless, even to the point of self-annihilation and ultimate separation from God himself. The JWT is not an adequate moral instrument to see us through the nuclear age.

The kingdom of Christ, the Lord

The JWT operates from assumptions that do not adequately take into account the vision of God's kingdom as manifested in Jesus Christ and the apostolic church. God entered the fray of human history to reverse the increase of violence and to establish a vision of peace. The substance of this vision involved establishing one community of God's people where peaceful living would provide an alternative to the injustice, violence, and warring of sinful humanity.

Thus in Jesus Christ, God entered into the brickyards of human society to reverse the curse of Cain and to release his people from bondage. In Jesus, God continues to be the warrior contending against the principalities and powers of evil. This Jesus resisted evil by loving the enemy and preaching the gospel of peace. He came to inaugurate a new kingdom, a new spiritual and social community of people.

Jesus Christ conquered the temptation to be an international leader, yet his new kingdom community ultimately posed a threat to the Roman Empire itself as it proclaimed, taught and imitated the way of the cross, the way of humility and service. This was the nonviolent way of Jesus who has absorbed and who will absorb the violence of the nuclear and revolutionary Cain. He was and is the supreme defense of us all. We look to his defenselessness on the cross as a model and to his resurrection as a source of power.

Jesus Christ as victor and victim stands with all the victims of humanity in the nuclear age and holds back doom while offering hope. Out of that victory Christians must call together a faithful remnant of God's people who will say a resounding "NO" to nuclear destruction. Such a people will bear witness to the fact that the very attitude which drives the nations toward nuclear war speaks a big "NO" to the gospel of Jesus Christ in our time and provides an occasion for God's judgment.

But the members of the kingdom of Christ must also resist frantic activity which simply draws people into a survivalist movement in the face of the nuclear threat. Likewise, they must resist a fatalistic pessimism that is resigned to accepting the inevitable. For the kingdom of God speaks a message of resurrection hope. Its members must call people everywhere to repentance for attitudes and actions that betray our rebellious nature. That is the mission of the church of Christ. It must speak and live a gospel that states that Jesus Christ is victor over the rebellious powers.

Christians must reckon with the day of the Bomb and the bullet, but they must not be overcome by it. We must pray that the evidence of Christ's triumph might be present even after such an unthinkable event. That will be the most difficult of all times to live the way of the cross. Yet the church will be called upon to suffer with the Lamb.

The War of the Lamb is the only justifiable war. All other wars only lead the human family deeper into the cycle of revenge and murder. The JWT has not been able to break that cycle. It has only led us more deeply into it. For it has not adequately understood the fundamental conflict between the kingdom of Christ and the kingdom of the anti-Christ, and the victory of the former over the latter. The only defense for Christians today is to continue to pray "thy kingdom come here on earth."

Wesley J. Prieb

Following the Flag of a New Kingdom

Missionary John C. Paton tells the story of how a converted island chief, full of the love of Christ, and four other Christian men responded when they were greeted with a shower of spears in a hostile island village. Addressing the villagers the Christian chief said, "We come to you without weapons of war! We come only to tell you about Jesus. We believe that he will protect us today." The villagers were so surprised at these Christians who came without weapons and even refused to throw the spears back, that they stopped fighting. Then the Christian chief spoke again: "Jehovah thus protects us. Once we would have thrown your spears back at you and killed you. He has changed our dark hearts. He asks you now to lay down all these other weapons of war, and to hear what we can tell you about the love of God, our Father, the only living God." The witness of the Christian chief and his four friends led the whole tribe to become Christians. Lamb power had overcome the hostile warriors.

William Blake (1757-1827), the British poet who wrote the poems "The Tiger" and "The Lamb," believed that love and forgiveness are the forces that bond the universe. He once said, reflecting on the love of Jesus, that "God became as we are that we may be as he is."

In "The Tiger" Blake is puzzled by the contradictory qualities of the lamb and the tiger, both created by God.

Tiger, Tiger, burning bright
in the forsts of the night,
What immortal hand or eye
Could frame thy fearful symmetry?

Blake asks a question pondered by many seekers of truth: "Did he who made the lamb make thee?"

Blake was more impressed by the lamb than the tiger. His conviction that humanity cannot survive without love, self sacrifice, and forgiveness prompts us to compare and contrast lamb power and tiger power, and then examine three pivotal expressions of lamb power in the Bible.

Ulysses and the Greek code of honor

Human nature and history reflect the tension between two ways of resolving conflict: tiger power and lamb power. Tiger power is easily understood and commonly practiced. It seems to be very logical. Conflicts are resolved by restraining, threatening, punishing or destroying the offender through physical force.

Tiger power was clearly defined by the ancient teacher of Greek civilization, Homer. His epic *Iliad* illustrates the code of honor.

The hero of the epic is Ulysses, the ideal Greek man, a warrior king, who acts the way all Greek men are expected to act when their honor is offended. The story describes how the Greeks avenged the abduction of Helen. The resolution of the conflict led to a ten-year war between the Greeks and the Trojans. The walled city of Troy in Asia Minor was sacked about 1200 B.C.

What was the cause of the war? Paris, son of Priam, the king of Troy, violated the Greek code of hospitality while visiting a Greek chieftan named Menelaus. Paris fell in love with his host's wife, Helen, eloped with her, and kept her in Troy.

Before Helen chose Menelaus as her husband, Helen had been courted by many Greek suitors, all of whom took an oath to sustain her choice of husband and avenge her cause if necessary. Ulysses, one of the Greeks who took the oath, later married Penelope, cousin of Helen. When Paris kidnapped Helen, the Greek chieftans, bound by their honor and oath, agreed to avenge Helen by attacking and destroying the Trojans and their city.

Ulysses was finally convinced by his comrades that he would have to leave his young bride and son and go to war. Justice demanded his involvement. The code of honor dictated that he join the Greek forces to recover Helen and her abductors.

After years of frustrated attempts to penetrate the fortified city, the Greeks finally achieved their goal through the ingenious trickery of Ulysses. The Greeks pretended to withdraw from the battle. They constructed an immense wooden horse, which they made out to be a propitiatory offering. But it was in fact filled with armed men. Then they hid behind some hills.

The Trojans, curious about the horse, opened the city gates, pulled the horse into the city walls, and then in a great festival celebrated the end of the war. During the night the armed man broke out of the horse and opened the gates of the city to their friends who had returned under the cover of night. The city was set on fire. The people, overcome with feasting and sleep, were killed. Helen was recovered. The conflict was resolved through the total destruction of the city.

Revenge of the tiger

The sacking of Troy was a just war in the eyes of Homer. Ulysses was honored as a great hero. Through his exceptional courage, wit, strength and military strategy the city was leveled and the enemy destroyed. Troy paid the price for her sins. The Greeks had been vindicated.

In this story we see a clear example of how tiger power works. It is defined by Homer as follows:

1. Pride is the key to human dignity and honor.
2. Revenge is a duty when honor is offended.
3. Security is provided by physical strength, courage, loyalty,

treasures and weapons.

4. Justice requires that the enemy must pay—suffer or die—for his sins.

5. Peace is achieved through the domination of tiger power—"the king of the mountain."

The code of honor has since been modified. The third party has been added to define the requirements of justice; trial by jury protects both the offended and offender; punishment of the offender is not the right of the offended; justice has become more important than honor.

Nevertheless, in many national disputes and often in private or domestic conflicts, tiger power prompts people to take the law in their own hands and they become both judge and executioner, motivated by revenge. The world still applauds the man who, when his honor is offended, deals with the offender in Homeric style.

Isaiah sees a suffering lamb

In Hebrew civilization, in contrast to the Greeks, God is seen as the judge and executioner. Though the Hebrew nation often acted like the Greeks, their prophets clearly taught: "Vengeance is mine, says the Lord."

The outcome of many of the wars in the Old Testament was determined not so much by the power of man but by the intervention of God (see chapter 5). God is the ruler of heaven and earth. The Hebrews learned more about mercy, forgiveness and self-sacrifice than the Greeks.

One of the great Hebrew teachers of the ancient world was Isaiah. Homer and Isaiah possibly lived at the same time, but one thing is clear: their teachings clashed. Isaiah defined for Israel a radically different kind of king. The Messiah who would come to lead Israel would be a lamb—not a tiger, wrote Isaiah in Isaiah 53:3-7:

> *He is despised and rejected of men; a man of sorrows, and acquainted with grief: and we hid as it were our faces from him; he was despised, and we esteemed him not.*

Surely he hath borne our griefs, and carried our sorrows; yet we did esteem him stricken, smitten of God, and afflicted.

But he was wounded for our transgression, he was bruised for our iniquities: the chastisement of our peace was upon him; and with his stripes we are healed.

All we like sheep have gone astray; we have turned every one to his own way; and the Lord hath laid on him the iniquity of us all.

He was oppressed, and he was afflicted, yet he opened not his mouth: he is brought as a lamb to the slaughter, and as a sheep before her shearers is dumb, so he openeth not his mouth.

How utterly absurd Isaiah's vision of the suffering lamb of God must have seemed to the Greeks and Hebrews alike. Lamb power always seems so terribly unworkable. *Yet through Jesus, the sacrificial lamb, we see manifested a power far greater than anything the world can offer us.*

Isaiah defines lamb power as follows:

1. Love is the basis for resolving conflict.

2. Forgiveness is a duty when sinned against.

3. Security is provided by trusting the shepherd.

4. Redemption requires that the sacrificial agent must pay—suffer or die—for the sins of the enemy.

5. Peace is achieved through non-violent lamb power—the suffering servant of the cross.

THREE ALTARS IN THE BIBLE

At the beginning of human history, before the fall, Adam and Eve lived in lamb-like peace with themselves and with the creatures of the earth. They didn't need to kill in order to live—God didn't create humans with claws, meat-tearing teeth, horns, or a stinger. Even the animals were lamblike, living together in peace and harmony.

But after the fall humans and beasts became tigerish. Humans didn't have the natural tools of warfare, but with their clever minds they quickly invented defensive and offensive killing weapons. It didn't take long before humans turned their weapons against each other.

In the first war of human history Cain killed his brother Abel, who was a shepherd. Cain's honor had been offended; his pride drove him to revenge. He tried to resolve a conflict by killing his brother.

Instead of resolving the conflict, Cain managed to get himself cursed and banished by God. In life he suffered more then his brother in death. That is the problem with tiger power. When you think the conflict is over, the trouble only begins.

The history of God's children would have ended quickly if the power of the lamb had not returned. Fallen humanity needed help. Paradise was lost. God had to find a way to save his people from self-destruction. His redemption strategy was centered in three great altars. The sacrificial lamb is part of each altar.

Saved by the blood of the lamb

The Passover was the most important celebration in the Old Testament. The annual festival focused the most important event in the history of Israel, the liberation of Israel from Egyptian bondage. Slavery was the issue. When Moses said to Pharaoh, "Let my people go," the Egyptian ruler said, "No, you will continue to be slaves." How was Israel liberated?

Moses couldn't believe his eyes when he stretched out his hands over the sea and saw the waters cover the chariots, the horsemen, and all the host of Pharoah. Moses knew very well that Israel had been saved not by military strategy or might, but by a miracle.

I will sing unto the Lord.
The Lord is my strength,
and he is become my salvation.

Israel, after her delivery, was commanded to observe the Passover each year. She must never forget that she had been saved by the blood of the lamb—the blood applied to the door posts and lintels, the blood which saved the first-born sons of Israel from the death angel which killed the first-born sons of Egypt.

Pharoah, the great tiger, couldn't cope with lamb power. How embarrassing for a mighty warlord to be overcome by the blood of the lamb.

Israel learned an important lesson too: the good shepherd cares for his sheep. Every year they were reminded during the Passover festival that they had been saved by the sacrificial lamb. The sacrifice became a powerful symbol God used to help his people understand the nature of his love.

Three characteristics of the lamb helped illustrate God's love and mercy:

(1) The lamb is vulnerable. It seems powerless and defenseless. It has no weapons to protect itself, thus the common expression of helplessness: "sheep among wolves."

(2) The lamb's only security is the shepherd. This is the secret of lamb power. Tigers, wolves, lions don't easily accept shepherds. This is why they fail in the end. Where are the lions and tigers today? A few are left in the jungle and zoos, where they are hunted or visited as a dying breed in modern civilization. Meanwhile the sheep have inherited the earth because they have the protection of a shepherd.

(3) The lamb sustains life. *In dying* it provides nutrition for humans and beast. Roasted lamb was eaten in generous quantities during sacrificial meals. *In dying* the lamb sheds its blood. Blood is the basis and key to life—thus its great symbolic value. Blood is a purifying agent. It is like a sponge which sucks up impurities.

In a symbolic way blood makes it possible for unholy men and women to commune with a holy God. The blood is a healing and reconciling agent in that it brings peace—peace defined as a right relationship between human beings and God.

Finally, *in dying* the lamb serves as a substitute. It takes upon itself the consequences of humanity's sin and thereby saves men and women from the law of the harvest. This is the basis of lamb power—taking punishment rather than dishing it out. The lamb saves human beings from their own self-destruction.

Behind the symbol of the lamb, of course, stands a loving and forgiving God who is ready at all times to be the shepherd of men and women. God promises to deliver and to save his people. All he wants in return is trust and obedience.

The winners are men and women; they haven't lost anything during the sacrifice except their pride and self-reliance. They gain everything as they surrender themselves to the shepherd of the sheep. *As men and women becomes part of God's covenant, they receive a new form of divine security that surpasses anything the world can offer or understand.*

Sacrifice not dominion

As all students of the Bible know, the sacrificial Passover lamb became the prototype of Jesus the Lamb of God. One of the first prophets to anticipate Jesus in the form of the suffering lamb was Isaiah in the passage cited earlier. When Jesus appeared, John the Baptist said, "Behold the Lamb of God which taketh away the sin of the world."

The great sacrificial altar of Christ, of course, was the cross; and this altar, which culminated in the Resurrection, is celebrated by Christians annually during the Easter season and regularly at the Lord's Table.

This cup is the new testament in my blood, which is shed for you (Luke 22:2).

Who in his own self bare our sins in his own body on the tree, that we, being dead to sins, should live unto righteousness: by whose stripes we were healed (1 Peter 2:23-25).

Having made peace through the blood of his cross, by him to reconcile all things unto himself (Colossians 1:20).

The good news of the gospel is that God took the initiative in redeeming fallen humanity by sending his Son, the lamb of God, as a sacrifice into the broken world to seek and to save that which was lost. As the begotten Son, Jesus showed forth God's love on the cross, the sacrificial altar:

He paid for humanity's sins...he did not condemn the sinners.
He forgave his enemies...he did not destroy them.
He suffered...he did not cause suffering.
He loved...he did not hate.
He died as the lamb of God and rose again...he did not kill.
He served through suffering love and self-sacrifice...he did not
seek dominion as a war lord.

At the very core of the redemptive process—the gospel of
salvation—is the principle of sacrifice. Forgiveness, mercy, and love
require vicarious suffering. The forgiving agent pays the price, and
the offender is rescued from the consequences of his own sins.

The disciple's altar

There is a third altar in the Bible which is not celebrated very
much. Yet is is an altar which believers cannot escape: the disciple's
cross of Matthew 16:24: "If any man will come after me let him deny
himself, and take up his cross and follow me."

The disciple's cross calls the follower of Jesus to exercise lamb
power, to be a sacrificial lamb. Paul says in Romans 12:1-2: "I appeal
to you therefore, brethren, by the mercies of God, to present your
bodies as a living sacrifice, holy and acceptable to God, which is
your spiritual worship."

The same self-sacrifice which is at the heart of Christ's atonement
operates in the cross of the disciple and the ministry of the church,
the visible body of Christ in the world. Through the divine love of
Christ the church offers itself vicariously to the world.

As Christ's extended body in history the church becomes broken
bread and sacrificial wine for the needs of the world. The power of
Christ in the church is the power to suffer martyrdom, not to inflict
it. The believer is called to become the salt of the earth, expending
self and giving self that the lost might be saved.

All people are invited to accept Christ's atonement on the cross
and then to accept responsibility as cross-bearing followers of Christ.
True evangelism embraces the method of the cross: Lamb Power,
God's way of bringing peace to humanity and God's way of sending

his ministers into the world as agents of reconciliation.

The call to this kind of lamb power, that is, peacemaking, is binding upon all followers of the suffering lamb of God.

> *Christ also suffered for us, leaving us an example, that ye should follow his steps (1 Peter 2:21).*

> *Be ye therefore followers of God, as dear children; and walk in love, as Christ also hath loved us (Ephesians 5:2).*

The lamb will win

Salvation is a gift of God's love. The sinner whom God forgives is saved, born again, radically turned around. He/she is now a "little Christ" who wants to do the will of the Shepherd. In simple lamb-like obedience he/she seeks to follow Christ and accepts the call of discipleship: "Take up your cross and follow me." In so doing he/she is at peace with God and other human beings.

He/she accepts Christ as Savior and Lord of life.

He/she obeys God rather than man.

He/she forgives... does not seek revenge.

He/she loves... does not hate.

He/she suffers... does not hurt or kill others.

He/she overcomes through suffering servanthood... does not seek dominion over others.

The redemption story ends with a great vision. John sees the culmination of history in a great celebration in which angels, the redeemed people of God, and the creatures honor the lamb as the triumphant king on the throne.

> *And every creature which is in heaven, and on earth, and under the earth, and such as are in the sea, and all that are in them, heard a voice saying, "Blessing and honor, and glory, and power, be unto him that sitteth upon the throne, and unto the lamb for ever and ever."*

John is making a promise—the lamb will win. The lamb has power, power to establish a kingdom of peace that will endure forever and ever. Isaiah too predicted that "The wolf and lamb shall feed together, and the lion shall eat straw." The lion and the wolf and the tiger will become lamblike—animals of peace. Lamb power will win. Paradise will be regained. This is the hope of every believer.

APPENDIX I

About the Authors

Mervin Dick is a former pastor of Mennonite Brethren Churches in Weatherford and Edmond, Oklahoma, Minneapolis, Minnesota, and Fresno, California, and is now the Mennonite Urban Minister in Denver, Colorado.

John Fast is an instructor of religious studies at Fresno Pacific College in Fresno, California. He is currently on study leave to complete a doctoral program in social ethics at Boston University.

Howard J. Loewen is a professor of theology at the Mennonite Brethren Biblical Seminary in Fresno, California. He also has taught at the Mennonite Brethren Bible College in Winnipeg, Manitoba, and Fresno Pacific College in Fresno.

Elmer A. Martens is the President and professor of Old Testament at the Mennonite Brethren Biblical Seminary in Fresno, California. Prior to his tenure at the Seminary he served as a pastor in Fresno.

Gordon Nickel is the former associate editor of the *Mennonite Brethren Herald,* the periodical of the Mennonite Brethren Churches of Canada. He is currently a student at the Mennonite Brethren Biblical Seminary in Fresno.

Wesley J. Prieb is Director of the Center for Mennonite Brethren Studies in Hillsboro, Kansas, and professor of English Literature at Tabor College in Hillsboro.

Henry J. Schmidt is a professor of evangelism and church growth and Director of the Center for Training in Mission/Evangelism at the Mennonite Brethren Biblical Seminary in Fresno, California. He also has served as a pastor in South Dakota and California.

John E. Toews is a professor of New Testament and the Academic Dean of the Mennonite Brethren Biblical Seminary. He also has taught at Fresno Pacific College in Fresno, Conrad Grebel College/University of Waterloo in Waterloo, Ontario, and Tabor College in Hillsboro, Kansas.

APPENDIX II

John E. Toews

Mennonite Brethren Statements on War and Peace in North America

1902, Confession of Faith (Glaubensbekenntnis, Halbstadt, Russia, pp. 48-50)

The first Mennonite Brethren Confession of Faith written and published in Russia taught the peace position.

> We believe and confess, according to the words of the Lord Jesus Christ: 'Ye have heard that it hath been said, An eye for an eye, and a tooth for a tooth: But I say unto you, that ye resist not evil. Love your enemies, bless them that curse you, do good to them that hate you, and pray for them which despitefully use you, and persecute you; that ye may be children of your Father which is in heaven; for He maketh His sun to rise on the evil and on the good, and sendeth rain on the just and on the unjust.' No one may practice revenge against his enemies. We also do not feel justified to carry the sword. The apostle Paul teaches thus. 'Dearly beloved, avenge not yourselves, but rather give place unto wrath; for it is written: Vengeance is mine; I will repay, saith the Lord. Therefore, if thine enemy hunger, feed him; if he thirst, give him drink; for in so doing thou shalt heap coals of fire on his head. Be not overcome of evil, but overcome evil with good.' The apostle Peter also says: 'For this is thankworthy, if a man for conscience toward God endure grief, suffering wrong-

fully. For what glory is it, if, when ye be buffeted for your faults, ye shall take it patiently? But if, when ye do well, and suffer for it, ye take it patiently, this is acceptable with God. For even hereunto were ye called; because Christ also suffered for us, leaving us an example, that we should follow His steps; who did not sin, neither was guile found in His mouth: who, when He was reviled, reviled not again; when He suffered, He threatened not; but committed Himself to Him that judgeth righteously. Matt. 5:21, 25, 28, 40, 48; 26:52-53; John 8:11; Rom. 12:19-21; I Pet. 2:19-23; I Cor. 6:1-8.

Translated from German into English in 1917 by H.F. Toews.

1916, Confession of Faith (Glaubensbekenntnis, Hillsboro, KS, pp. 43-45)

The 1902 Confession from Russia was published in German in the United States.

1917, Confession of Faith (Hillsboro, KS, pp. 42-44)

The 1902 Confession as published in the US in 1916 was translated into English by H.F. Toews and published for the churches in North America.

1917, Southern District Conference Resolution, Enid, OK, October 14-16 (Southern District Conference Yearbook, hereafter (SDCY, p.49)

Following a report on a Mennonite delegation visit to Washington, D.C., the Conference resolved that:

> We can render any service outside the military establishment, which aims to support and save life; but we cannot participate in any work which will result in personal injury or loss of life to others. Consequently, we can do such work as is at present assigned to non-combatants in Camp Funston and Camp Travis only under protest, because it appears that such service virtually constitutes military service, since the work is required by the military authorities and must be done within the military establishment.

1919, General Conference Resolution, Mountain Lake, MN, November 3-5 (GCY, pp. 48-49)

The Conference meeting in the aftermath of World War I felt the interpretative comment in the 1902 Confession, "we also do not feel justified to carry the sword," was too weak and needed to be strengthened. Therefore, the Conference agreed to delete this sentence and to add the following paragraph to the Confession of Faith:

> For on the matter of war we believe and confess, that the way it is waged by the western powers, it is manifestly contrary to the principle of the kingdom of Christ, and therefore our members are forbidden to participate in it. We much more have to wage a spiritual warfare against the powers of darkness, that rule in the air. 'For we wrestle not against flesh and blood, but against principalities, against powers, against the rulers of the darkness of this world, against spiritual wickedness in high places' (Eph. 6:12). And Jesus says: 'Put up again thy sword into its place; for all they that take the sword shall perish with the sword' (Mt. 26:52). 'Know ye not what manner of spirit ye are of? For the Son of man is not come to destroy men's lives, but to save them' (Lk. 9:55-56). 'My kingdom is not of this world: if my kingdom were of this world, then would my servants fight, that I should not be delivered to the Jews; but now is my kingdom not from hence' (Jn. 18:36). And the Apostle Paul says (2 Cor. 10:3-6), 'For though we walk in the flesh, we do not war after the flesh: For the weapons of our warfare are not carnal, but mighty through God to the pulling down of strongholds: Casting down imaginations, and every high thing that exalteth itself against the knowledge of God, and bringing into captivity every thought to the obedience of Christ; And having in a readiness to revenge all disobedience, when your obedience is fulfilled.'

> Therefore we take our stand with Peter and the other Apostles. We ought to obey God rather than man (Acts 5:29).

1921, Southern District Conference Resolution, Ebenfeld, KS, October 15-19 (SDCY, pp. 40-42)

The Conference agreed to designate a day of prayer one week prior to November 11 to pray for an international conference on disarmament to be held in Washington, to encourage individual church members to write President Harding endorsing disarmanent, to authorize the Conference leadership to write President Harding a letter fully supporting disarmament, and to encourage disarmament through periodic sermons in the churches and articles in the Conference periodicals.

1921, Central District Conference Resolution, Henderson, NE, October 22-25 (CDCY, pp. 19-20)

The Conference agreed to 1) call all the churches to a time of prayer for disarmament on Sunday, November 6; 2) encourage individuals to write personal letters to Congressional representatives and senators to encourage support for disarmament; 3) authorize the chairman and secretary of the Conference to write the President of the United States a letter supporting efforts toward disarmament.

1922, Southern District Conference Resolution, Boyd, OK, October 15-17 (SDCY, pp. 58-60)

Three brothers, G. Wiens, H.H. Flaming, H.W. Lohrenz, reported on a Peace Church conference on disarmament in Bluffton, Ohio. They felt some representatives were advocating political involvement to abolish war in the world. The three brothers presented the following resolution to the Conference as a Mennonite Brethren response to the peace conference:

> The motivation for this conference, as we understand it, was to bring about a warless world. But we believe that such a world cannot come to pass until the Prince of Peace, the Lord Jesus Christ Himself, comes again.
>
> Nevertheless we believe first of all that it is our obligation to proclaim the word of peace in our walk in the home, in the Sunday School, in the church and in the neighborhood.
>
> Secondly, we accept our obligation to maintain our position toward our government, as it is outlined in Jer. 29:7 and 1 Tim. 2:1. This includes that we try to influence our government, especially the Congress, to maintain the peace and to avoid war.
>
> We believe that our greatest mission is to proclaim the gospel of salvation which leads to the renewal of the inner man, for without being born from above enduring peace cannot be attained (Rom. 12:1,2; 8:1, 2, 5, 6; Gal. 5:6ff.).

Our position is clearly stated in the Confession of Faith.

We do not think that this conference was in vain, even though we could not agree with parts of the program. Such conferences are a valuable stimulation and preparation in that they contribute to the following:

1. They spur us and our youth to lead a Christian life through which the divine light can shine.

2. They serve to unite us in our position in the event of war. What is our position in regard to the forced bearing of arms, to wearing the uniform, to the kinds of service our young men can perform?

3. They offer new opportunities to unite our energies in the alleviation of the distress and destruction created by war, pestilence and accidents.

The Conference approved the resolution, and encouraged the men to continued participation in such conferences.

1934, Northern District Conference (the earlier name for the Canadian Conference), Winkler, MB, June 30-July 4 (NDCY, pp. 76-77)

Two resolutions were presented to the Canadian Conference, the first by the Rosthern District Conference(SK). It requested the Canadian Conference to address the nonresistance question with the government during peace time in order to insure the rights of the Mennonite Brethren in case of war. The second resolution, presented by the Russian Mennonite Church and the Evangelical Christian Baptists acting in concert, asked the Mennonite Brethren Church to join them in an anti-war resolution which would refuse any form of support for war.

The Conference responded to these resolutions by 1) rejecting the anti-war resolution; 2) affirming the peace position and the importance of teaching it in the churches; 3) initiating contacts with the Canadian Government to insure the non-participation of Mennonite Brethren in war; 4) electing a Committee to open conversation with other peace churches in Canada and to work with the US Mennonite Brethren Committee on Defenselessness.

1934, Pacific District Conference Resolution, Reedley, CA, November 5-7 (PDCY, p. 27)

The Conference was informed by the General Conference Committee on Nonresistance that the Supreme Court of the United States had ruled that "every citizen must bear arms for the defense of the United States."

The Conference requested the General Conference Committee on Nonresistance to open negotiations with the government for noncombatant service in the event of war, and to explore with other peace churches how they were responding to the decision of the Supreme Court.

1935, Northern District Conference Resolution, Main Centre, SK, July 7-10 (NDCY, pp. 49-54)

The Committee on Defenselessness, appointed at the 1934 Conference, reported that Canadian law permits non-participation in military service for persons whose confession of faith is opposed to participation in war. The Committee recommended that the Mennonite Brethren Church make representation to the Canadian Government together with other peace churches to clarify the position of the Mennonite Churches. The Committee further observed that of all the teachings in the confession of faith the position of nonresistance is the most neglected one. Therefore, it suggested more teaching and writing in the conference periodical to educate members of the church. The Conference approved the recommendation.

1935, Southern District Conference Resolution, Buhler, KS, October 19-22 (SDCY, pp. 30-31)

P.R. Lange and P.C. Hiebert, Conference leaders, raised the question of possible cooperation with the Quakers for peace teachings and alternative service work. The Conference resolved that

> the Committee on Nonresistance get in touch immediately with the brethren who had been in the camps, and listen to their counsel for a plan for mutual work on this question. As soon as the plan was completed it should be published in the Conference

paper. The matter should not be delayed, but be pursued energetically with the help of God so that we as a brotherhood are prepared to take a united stand in case of a war.

1936, Northern District Conference Resolution, Waldheim, SK, July 4-8 (NDCY, pp. 79-81)

The Conference, aware of preparations for war in the world, resolved 1) to affirm the principle of nonresistance and service, even sacrificial service to preserve life; 2) to appoint a committee to represent Mennonite Brethren concerns to the government together with representatives from other Mennonite churches; 3) to work vigorously in teaching the younger generation the principle of nonresistance through proclamation and writing.

1936, Southern District Conference Resolution, Fairview, OK, October 24-28 (SDCY, p. 139)

The Southern District Committee on Defenselessness presented a resolution to the Conference outlining the Mennonite Brethren position on war and peace. The resolution is the identical one presented to the General Conference, November 21-26 (see next resolution). The District Conference approved the resolution for presentation to the General Conference.

1936, General Conference Resolution, Reedley, CA, November 21-26 (GCY, pp. 60-63)

The Committee on the War Question, appointed between the 1933 and 1936 General Conferences, proposed a three point resolution based on study of Scripture, examination of "the viewpoints of other like-minded denominations," and the testing "of most of our leading brethren."

1. Our position on war

We gratefully remember the fact that we belong to a people and to a church which historically condemns war and advocates peace. We would briefly like to make our current position on this issue known to the world.

As a Mennonite Brethren Church we declare our opposition to war in any form and our determination to practice peace and love.

The basis for this position is outlined in the following:

a) The principles of peace are rooted in Christ and his word.

b) Through faith we have become partakers of the Spirit and the character of our Lord and Savior and through this it is mandatory to love all people, even our enemies.

c) Christ has shown us the worth of the human soul in his words and example, by telling and showing us that everyone can become a child of God.

d) The spirit of self-denying service, of love and of mutual goodwill promote the greatest welfare of mankind. Whereas the spirit of hate, jealousy and fear destroys the best and most noble in man. The history of mankind verifies this.

e) War is sin. It stands in direct opposition to the Spirit of Christ, to Christian love, indeed to everything Christ represents. War is wrong in its spirit and method which results in destruction. Therefore it is impossible for us to take part in war, in the struggle between nations, between classes or between individual persons.

f) Our highest and first civic duty is towards our God and our Lord. We are resolved to follow Christ in all respects and therefore we cannot take on obligations, which in essence and purpose stand in contradiction to Christ. We also believe we are doing our country the best service in this way and declare ourselves genuinely loyal to our nation.

2. Our Understanding of Patriotism

The members of the Mennonite Brethren Church love our country and are truly striving to seek the country's wellbeing to the best of their ability. True love for our country does not demand hate towards another country. It is our conviction that the practice of the principles of peace, love, justice, liberty and national and international goodwill serve towards the highest good for our country as well as that of all mankind. Our faith promises security through love and protection, through acts of goodwill and justice. For these we are ready to make the necessary sacrifices.

We do not refuse to enter military service to gain personal advantages or to draw a less dangerous lot in times of war. We choose it because we consider any activity which destroys or causes loss of human life as unjust and contrary to true discipleship of the Prince of Peace.

We are against war as a means of settling differences because war is unchristian, it destroys, it works in opposition to the highest and noblest values of man and because it sows the seeds of future wars. We are convinced that we are true patriots with this stand because we represent the eternal principles of justice, on which alone a stable government is possible.

3. Recommendations to our brethren of the faith

1. That the leading servants of each church be diligent to give information to all its members concerning our position on war.
2. That all church members prove themselves as children of peace by refusing to accept any service that has the destruction of property as its objective, that seeks to end or cause the end of human life, or that be contrary to their conscientious scruples.
3. That we do not hide our light under a bushel but demonstrate our convictions of peace and clarify the basic reasons for it.
4. That in view of the threatening world situation we inform our young men how to conduct themselves in the event of war.

The Conference approved the resolution.

1937, Northern District Conference Resolution, Winkler, MB, July 3-7 (NDCY, pp. 60-61)

After being reminded that Canadian law recognizes nonresistance for conscience reasons, the Conference resolved to 1) prepare and circulate literature on the peace position; 2) use youth meetings to educate young people to the peace teachings of the Bible; 3) recommend that each District Conference appoint a brother to visit the churches to teach nonresistance.

The Conference cautioned against the use of existing pacifist literature that was based on political or radical assumptions. All literature used in the church should base nonresistance on biblical teachings, the Conference exhorted.

1937, Southern District Conference Resolution, Hillsboro, KS, October 23-26 (SDCY, pp. 51-52)

The Conference, following receipt of a report on a Peace Church meeting with President Roosevelt, passed the following resolution to encourage the teaching and the practice of the peace position in the churches:

> 1. Every worker in the Kingdom of God shall study in order to be well grounded and faithful, and also ready to bear witness.
> 2. Every father and mother shall teach their children the necessity of taking a position against war and bloodshed.
> 3. The Conference shall designate November 11 as Peace Sunday, and all the churches shall observe this Sunday. The sermon and every aspect of the service shall focus on peace and oppose war.
> 4. Every church member shall strive earnestly and consistently to live the doctrine of peace.

1937, Pacific District Conference Resolution, Reedley, CA, November 26-28 (PDCY, p. 37)

The Conference adopted the identical resolution to the Southern District one above.

1938, Northern District Conference Resolution, Winnipeg, MB, July 2-6 (NDCY, pp. 54-55)

The Conference was informed that literature on the peace position was being prepared in cooperation with the US Churches, and would be made available in both German and English.

The Conference resolved that 1) fathers in the home and church leaders commit themselves to set a good example in word and deed regarding the peace teaching; 2) the Conference recognize that the deepening of the peace conviction in a time of world-wide preparation for war was one of the most important responsibilities of the church; 3) the churches make the peace witness a matter of earnest prayer; 4) all the churches be asked to take one offering per year to support the distribution of peace literature.

1938, Central District Conference Resolution, Dolton, SD, October 1-4 (CDCY, pp. 29-30)

The Committee on Defenselessness recommended that in the event of war the members of the church encourage their young men to volunteer for services that are not in opposition to the teaching of the Bible and that contribute to the saving of life. The Committee also recommended that more be done to teach the young people the foundations of the faith.

The Conference responded by recommending that all the churches of the District set aside the Sunday before Armistice Day as Peace Sunday. It is expected, the resolution continued, that a sermon be preached on nonresistance from all pulpits which asserts that nonresistance is the belief of the church in times of war and in everyday life. The Conference also resolved that a brother be asked to visit all the churches of the District in the interests of nonresistance.

1938, Pacific District Conference Report, Bakersfield, CA, November 25-27 (PDCY, pp. 31-32)

The Conference received the report from the General Conference Committee on Nonresistance. The report exhorted the Conference as follows:

> Should war break out, we, who profess nonresistance, should encourage our young brethren to register for service that will not be contrary to the teaching of the Bible and in branches of service that save life.
>
> In this time more should be done to inform our people and others that war can never be reconciled with Bible teaching, and is completely opposed to Christ's teaching.

1939, Northern District Conference Resolution, Coaldale, AB, July 8-12 (NDCY, pp. 61-63)

The Committee on the War Question reported on three important peace conferences earlier in the year, a conference of all Mennonites in Canada and the US, a conference of the peace churches—Mennonites, Brethren, Quakers—in Chicago, and a conference of the Mennonites in Canada. The Mennonites together with the other peace churches, the Committee indicated, stand firm on the principle of non-participation in war and military service. Some of these groups also condemn alternative service, while others are willing to serve the state through health services.

The Committee requested counsel on whether the Mennonite Brethren should participate in the Inter-Mennonite Pilot Committee that was being formed in Canada. The Committee wanted it understood that any participation with pacifist groups whose foundation for the peace position was not biblical would be declined.

The Conference responded to the report by resolving 1) that alternative service in health care be under civilian control and that no weapons be carried by Mennonites in such service; 2) that the Mennonite Brethren participate in the Inter-Mennonite Committee; 3) that the Mennonite Brethren Church withdraw from the Inter-Mennonite Committee if it established links with "pacifistic, social-political organizations;" 4) that the Inter-Mennonite Committee should negotiate with the government if the latter should recommend nonmilitary forms of service other than health services; 5) that strong teaching on the peace position should be continued in the churches; 6) that a day of fasting and prayer for renewal of commitment to the peace position be observed in all the churches.

1939, Central District Conference Resolution, Henderson, NE, October 14-17 (CDCY, pp. 88-89)

Following a report on conversations with other peace churches the Conference resolved that 1) in the event of registration for war the young men of the church should register, but indicate they are nonresistant and willing to perform nonmilitary work; 2) if mobilization shall take place the young men should report that they are not willing to perform military work or service, and to request service in accord with the law of the land; 3) a plan be presented to the President of the United States outlining nonmilitary work that Mennonite young men would be willing to perform under civilian supervision; 4) the Conference recognize that the nonresistance position was bought with blood, and that it is important to demonstrate that Christians love each other and their enemies.

1939, General Conference Resolution, Corn, OK, October 21-25 (GCY, pp. 48-51)

The Conference, very much aware of world conditions and fearful of American involvement in the European war, agreed

(a) That the Committee on Nonresistance prepare a written document clarifying our position, and to enable us to present something specific if called on. (b) That we as Conference approve the organization of Mennonite Central Peace Committee and our participation in it. (c) That the proposed plan in the interests of the drafted youth be approved. (d) That the entire matter be worked out with the head of the nation, and be submitted for adoption as soon as practically possible. (e) That we put forth further efforts to teach the members of our church the way of peace, (1) through sermon and instruction in the home and in all worship services; (2) through the distribution of appropriate literature; (3) through the preparation of reports and addresses that elucidate this endeavor. (f) That by way of instruction and intercession we continue to observe the Sunday before Armistice Day as Peace Sunday, and in that connection gather an offering for the promotion of the peace movement. (g) That we counsel our youth that is subject to draft to accept service which helps to preserve life and rehabilitate property, if such service can be rendered under civilian administration, namely, outside the military organization. (h) That we counsel our members to remain humble but firm in their position of faith, even at the cost of suffering and persecution. To suffer for the faith is no disgrace, and promises reward for time and eternity.

In addition the Conference agreed to the following:

1. To encourage young men who may be drafted for military service to declare themselves Conscientious Objectors willing to perform other services.

2. To encourage individual men who may be drafted for military service to declare that it is impossible for them to perform military service but that they would be willing to perform nonmilitary service.

3. To join an Inter-Mennonite delegation for a meeting with the President of the United States to negotiate a Christian service program that would give expression to the peace position for the Mennonites and to bear witness to the gospel.

1941, Northern District Conference Resolution, Herbert, SK, July 5-7 (NDCY, pp. 51-56)

Following the presentation of a "treatise" on the biblical basis of the peace position by B.B. Janz, the Conference expressed concern about two issues: 1) the possibility that the health services form of alternative service might be removed from civilian control, and 2) that many young men had failed the National War Service Board test for health services and now faced the prospect of noncombatant service and military drill. The Conference authorized the Committee on the War Question to take whatever steps necessary to insure that young men who refused military drill for conscience reasons be permitted to do their service in parks, on highways or in civilian sanitariums.

1942, Central District Conference Resolution, Carson, MN, June 6-9 (CDCY, pp. 15-16)

The question was raised on the Conference floor about the purchase of "Defense Bonds." Following a discussion of alternatives, the Conference resolved 1) to thank God for the freedom enjoyed in the United States, to pledge loyalty to the government for permitting Mennonite Brethren young men to serve the country without contradicting the teachings of the Scripture and their consciences, and to pray for the leaders of the country; 2) to observe the Sunday following Armistice Day as a day of repentance, prayer and fasting to pray for the government, for the men in Civilian Public Service camps, and for the intensification of commitment to the peace position in the churches; 3) to give evidence of loyalty to the government by purchasing "Civilian Bonds" as soon as they are available; 4) to invite P.C. Hiebert to visit the churches in the interest of nonresistance and relief for war victims.

1942, Pacific District Conference Resolution, Shafter, CA, October 23-24 (PDCY, p. 48)

The Conference responded to a question about members working in shipyards and other defense projects by resolving that "in view of the fact that the government is offering a number of avenues of service wherein our faith is not violated, therefore we recommend that our members serve our government in these capacities."

1943, General Conference Resolution, Buhler, KS, May 26-30 (GCY, p. 67)

In the middle of World War II and in the context of a positive report on alternative service, the Conference resolved,

> 1. That we continue humbly grateful to our Heavenly Father for the many blessings that we enjoyed in the past as well as for the privileges what we enjoy today, namely, to live and teach what we believe to be the true will of God as expressed in His precious Word in accord with our stand as an historic peace church under the protection of our country and its constitution.
>
> 2. That we confirm our undivided loyalty to our country and our government which has graciously provided ways and means of affording our young men a chance to serve their country without being compelled to become a part of the military power which would be contrary to our confession of faith and their conscience.

1945, Northern District Conference Resolution, Yarrow, BC, June 16-21 (NDCY, p. 144)

A question was submitted to the Conference inquiring what could be done to better understand and practice the Confession of Faith, especially the teaching on nonresistance.

The Committee of Reference and Counsel expressed regret that many Mennonite Brethren sons and their families have forsaken the path of nonresistance. The Counsel suggested that this departure from "the convictions of our fathers" was not exclusively the fault of the young men, but also was due to the lack of teaching and modeling of the teaching in the church. Therefore, the Counsel recommended that all churches provide relevant literature, that church leaders teach Biblical nonresistance, and that believers live the principles of nonresistance in everyday life.

1945, General Conference Resolutions, Dinuba, CA, November 24-29 (GCY, pp. 40, 75)

The Conference passed two resolutions which opposed postwar conscription. The first stated "that we ask our brethren in the Public Relations Committee to lead us in exercising proper influence against peace time conscription of our young men, but that in case of its inevitable enactment, we favor asking for special provisions of service in a nonmilitary capacity." The second asserted "that the Mennonite Brethren Church of North America go on record as being opposed to any type of military conscription and that this decision be sent to Congress and the proper (other) authorities through Brother P.C. Hiebert."

1946, Canadian Conference Resolution, Winkler, MB, June 29-July 4 (CCYB, 1946, pp. 163-164)

Three questions were brought to the Conference for counsel. The first asked about how the peace position could be taught more clearly in the churches. The Conference asked H.H. Janzen and J.B. Toews to publish an explanation on the fundamental truths of the Mennonite Brethren Confession of Faith, and J.A. Toews, C.D. Toews, C.C. Peters, and I. Thiessen to visit the churches for the purpose of teaching the Confession of Faith, especially the teaching on non-resistance.

The second question inquired about what position Mennonite Brethren Churches should take toward men who served in the military and were returning to the churches. The Conference asserted that men returning from military service owed the church a statement of clarification. If they acknowledge that their decision was contrary to the principle of Mennonite Brethren faith and if they repent of their departure from the faith, the church should extend to them the hand of fellowship.

The third question concerned the baptism of persons who did not affirm the teaching of nonresistance. The Conference resolved that "we accept nonresistance as a special emphasis within our Confession of Faith and we obligate all persons baptized into the church to accept this teaching."

1947, Central District Conference Resolution, Marion, SD, October 11-15 (CDCY, p. 27)

The Conference agreed in the context of a review of post-war relief and peace concerns "that all pastors propogate with special effort the ministry of peace and nonresistance now in time of peace, and that if we should face another crisis, our members are able to take a firm stand to give a clear testimony to the Prince of Peace."

1947, Southern District Conference Resolution, Fairview, OK, October 25-29 (SDCY, pp. 59-60)

The Conference went on record

that all pastors and Sunday School teachers propagate with diligence the ministry of peace for which we are called, which should help prepare all of us and especially the young men to stand firmly by the faith of our fathers and of the Christian's religion and to give a clear testimony for the Prince of Peace at all times, and especially in the event of the impending crisis of another conflict.

The Conference also asked

that our church anew go on record as standing firmly against universal military training now advocated by many of our leading men in the government. And should military training be required, that we then ask for and accept alternative service independent of the military forces and under civilian direction as tentatively suggested in the proposed bill which will be introduced in Congress before long.

1947, Pacific District Conference Resolution, Dinuba, CA, November 22-25 (PDCY, p. 35)

The Conference spoke to two issues. First, it adopted the October Central District Resolution that all pastors should teach the peace position.

Secondly, it adopted the resolution against universal military training approved the month earlier by the Southern District Conference.

1948, Canadian Conference Resolution, Port Dalhousie, ON, July 3-8 (CCY, pp. 101-103)

The Conference adopted the following statement presented by the Committee of Reference and Counsel:

We regret that some members in our churches do not practice nonresistance in their personal lives, but want to be nonresistant in times of war. Such inconsistent Christian living beclouds our Christian witness in the world, and causes our young people to reject the teaching of nonresistance which we believe in our churches. For this reason we recommend that the following principles guide our faith in our church and personal lives;

1. We bow deeply before our Lord and Master, who has bought us at such a great price, that we have not learned to be more faithful to him in word and walk despite the much grace he has extended to us.

2. We confess that we as a Conference have been unfaithful to the ethical teachings of the Sermon on the Mount. We have been involved in activities and movements which do not preserve human life, but rather destroy it.

3. The Conference exhorts our churches to pray earnestly to God for revival among our members. Conflict, mistrust and all slander should be banned in our midst.

4. Every church should assume responsibility to teach its youth the principle of nonresistance. It should be emphasized that nonresistance does not only apply in war, but also in family, church and community life. It is possible to kill another person with the tongue.

5. Our churches need to have clear principles which can be followed in the event that God permits another catastrophe to occur in the world. Every brother in the church needs to know that if he participates in military service he terminates his membership in the church, and can be received back only on the basis of full repentance for his sin.

6. The Conference believes that many of our young men will find it difficult during a time of war to perform service that seems unimportant and meaningless, and that does not satisfy the feelings of obligation of their fellow citizens in the country.

For this reason the Conference should take definite steps now already to insure service in sanitariums and to maintain the alternative service system. The Conference should elect a Committee of three brethren to be sure that this work is done.

7. The Conference expresses its heartfelt thanks to the young men who bore such clear testimony to the confession of nonresistance in the last war. It prays that they will continue to serve their Lord and Master faithfully as nonresistant Christians.

8. The Conference knows that once false steps are taken they cannot be changed. Therefore, the Conference exhorts individuals and churches which took a false step in the last war to accept the costly Word of God in I John 1:9: 'If we confess our sins, he is faithful and just, and will forgive our sins and cleanse us from all unrighteousness.' As Jesus said to the woman caught in adultery, 'Go and sin no more' (John 8:1-11).

May God help us to take this matter more seriously and to desire to walk in his ways in order that we may glorify his name.

1948, General Conference Resolution, Mountain Lake, MN, August 28-September 2 (GCY, pp. 103-104)

The Board of General Welfare and Public Relations, the successor to the Committee on Nonresistance, asked the Board of Reference and Counsel to formulate a statement on the question of nonresistance. The occasion for the question was the insistence from several Canadian delegates that noncombatant service within the military be considered an acceptable expression of the peace position. The Board of Reference and Counsel presented the following statement:

> The Committee of Reference and Counsel deeply regrets that we have brethren in our churches who do not live according to the teaching of Jesus and the Apostles in their personal life, but in times of war desire to be non-resistant. Such inconsistent Christian living darkens our testimony before the world and causes our young people to look upon the principle of non-resistance which we confess in our churches, negatively and with disdain. We must again become clear and sound in this principle; therefore, the Committee of Reference and Counsel of the General Conference recommends the following fundamental principle for adoption:

1. That we humble ourselves deeply before our Lord and Master who has purchased us with His own life's blood, because we have not yet learned, inspite of all the grace bestowed upon us, to serve Him more faithfully in word and deed.

2. We confess that we, as a Conference, have in the past come far short of the ethical requirements and demands of the teachings of Jesus and the Apostles. We have often participated in activities and had our interests in movements that did not contribute to the preservation of human life: on the contrary, they often contributed to the destruction of life.

3. We recommend to the Conference and to the churches to pray sincerely for a spiritual revival in our denomination: quarrels, mistrust, deception, etc., must be banned from our midst.

4. That every church assume the obligation to instruct her young people in this fundamental principle of our faith—non-resistance. May we emphasize though, that non-resistance does not only concern itself with the bearing of arms but also with the life in the home, in the church, and in the neighborhood. It is also possible to destroy life with our tongue.

5. The Conference expects that our men eligible for service, whenever called upon, will render valuable service for our people and country in two channels according to their conscientious convictions:

a. In agriculture and forestry projects, mental hospitals, and other institutions of civilian character, and in the field of rehabilitation and relief.

b. As non-combatants in the medical corps, not bearing arms nor participating in the training with weapons, rendering the saving of lives, but not participating in any service that would tend toward the destruction of human life, and no service in defense plants. Arrangements should be made with the government at this time in order that such a way for service in the medical corps may be found. Under no circumstances can our brethren take the military oath. Their sincere affirmation will be sufficient.

6. Our brethren who have so faithfully lived their convictions during the last war and stood so soundly upon our principles of peace hereby receive the heartfelt appreciation and

sincere thanks of the Conference, and we pray that they may continue humbly in the service of their Lord and Master.

7. The above principles point out the direction for the future but do not react to the recent past where we have so seriously neglected to definitely point out the way by word and example. Humbly we bow ourselves under the Word of John 1:9, 'But if we confess our sins, he is faithful and just to forgive us our sins and to cleanse us from all unrighteousness.' Another word of God says, 'Go and sin no more.' God help us—we can do nothing else.

The 1948 resolution is noteworthy on two counts. First, the original resolution recommended that church members who do not agree with the Conference peace position be excluded from membership. This statement was deleted by Conference vote. Secondly, it recognized a noncombatant role within the military as an acceptable expression of the peace witness as long as it did not involve destruction of life, work in defense plants and the profession of the military oath.

1948, Southern District Conference Resolution, Hillsboro, KS, October 16-19 (SDCY, p. 55)

The Conference voted to affirm the resolution on the peace position accepted by the General Conference earlier in the year. Therefore, it "resolved that we reaffirm our stand as an historic Peace Church and encourage our young men to register in obedience to the law, but that they witness for our established faith by filling out the blank for conscientious objectors."

1948, Pacific District Conference Resolution, Bakersfield, CA, October 23-27 (PDCY, pp. 2-3, 41, 62)

The Conference opened with the presentation of a statement by the Reedley Church:

Whereas the 1948 Draft Act places the Historic Peace Churches anew before the responsibility of testifying to the principle of nonresistance, and whereas our General Conference has reaffirmed its position on this principle as contained in our 'Confession of Faith,' we recommend to our churches: 1. That we, as a local church, also reaffirm our position as a nonresistant church, who consider it sin to take part in the destruction of human life. 2. That we, as a church, assume the obligation to instruct our young people in this fundamental principle of our faith—nonresistance. We emphasize though, that nonresistance does not only concern itself with the bearing of arms but also with the life in the home, in the church, and in the neighborhood. It is also possible to destroy life with our tongue or other actions and attitudes. 3. That we, as loyal citizens of our country, are prepared to discharge our obligation for the welfare of our country in the form of an alternative Civilian Public Service or in noncombatant service preferably in the medical division of the army, as far as it deals exclusively with the preservation of human life. 4. The church considers it essential to recognize its responsibility for the discipline of members who violate the principle of nonresistance; either of those of the church membership at large or those who may choose to enter the combatant service. 5. That we, as a local church, kindly request that the Western District Conference, which is to convene in Bakersfield on October 22-26, clarify its stand as a Conference to the last point of this resolution.

The Conference responded to the Reedley statement in two ways. First of all, the Conference accepted a resolution from the Board of Welfare and Public Relations that "we reaffirm our stand as an historic Peace Church and encourage our young men to register in obedience to the law, but that they witness for our established faith by filling out the blank for conscientious objectors," and that "we support the work of alternative service with other members of the Mennonite Central Committee." The Conference reaffirmed the peace stance of the church, but also rejected noncombatant service as a valid expression of the peace witness. Secondly, the question about disciplinary action was referred to the next Ministers and Deacons Conference. No records of the latter Conference are available.

1949, Central District Conference Resolution, Munich, ND, June 11-15 (CDCY, p. 25)

Following a discussion of peace and relief concerns, the Conference passed two resolutions:

(1) We recommend that we are thankful to the Lord for the peace we have in the world today and that we in the coming year again set aside a Sunday as a Peace Emphasis Sunday, where we thank the Lord for the peace we enjoy and give a clear testimony of our faith in peace with God and all men.

(2) We recommend to our churches to give their full support to the peace teams that MCC will send to the various churches in the summer months to give a testimony to our belief in peace and nonresistance.

1950, Canadian Conference Resolutions, Abbotsford, BC, July 29-August 3 (CCY, pp. 98, 120-123)

The Conference spoke to the question of peace and nonresistance in three different ways.

First, the Youth Committee recommended that "in light of the current world situation, the churches intensify the teaching of our confession regarding the oath and nonresistance among the young people."

Secondly, the Committee on Nonresistance reported on three recent peace church meetings (Kitchener, Winnipeg, Detroit). The Detroit meeting was especially illuminating for the Mennonite Brethren. It was attended by 470 delegates from 15 denominations, the Committee reported. Many of these denominations, the report noted, had opposed nonresistance in the past, but were now open to this teaching. "What happened in Detroit," the Committee commented, "has never happened before in church history. While the teachings of nonresistance are fading in some Mennonite homes and churches, a new movement is arising committed to the way of peace. Therefore, the Mennonite and Mennonite Brethren churches should wake up and strengthen what is about to die or the Lord will destroy our candlestick and find other witnesses." The Committee reminded the Conference that all who enter military service terminate their relationship with the church. The Conference accepted the Committee's two major recommendations: a) to negotiate with the government now during peace time through an Inter-Mennonite delegation to guarantee that medical service within the military be limited to preserving life and not destroying life, and that no military training be involved in such medical service; b) that all families pray earnestly with their young people for clarity regarding nonresistance.

Thirdly, the Conference responded to a submitted question which asked that nonresistance be made "a church rule" binding on all members entering the church, by recommending that each baptismal candidate be given a Mennonite Brethren Confession of Faith and be taught the contents of the Confession in special instructional meetings.

1951, General Conference Resolution, Winkler, MB, July 21-26 (GCY, pp. 123-124)

The 1951 Conference amended the 1948 statement in two ways. First it voted to delete the sentence "their sincere affirmation will be sufficient" at the conclusion of paragraph 5b regarding the military oath for noncombatants. In other words, noncombatants within the military are not to take the military oath in any form. Secondly, the Conference added a third statement to paragraph 5 which declared participation in military service that destroyed life to be unbiblical and grounds for excommunication from the church. The additional paragraph reads as follows:

> That such as enter the Military Service to participate in the work that destroys human life, shall be considered as disobeying Principles of Scripture and our Confession of Faith and in consequence can no longer be considered members in good standing. It shall be our duty to continue to love them and make them the object of our intercessory prayers as erring brethren who must be sought in an effort to bring them back into the obedience of the Word of God. Such as refuse to obey the due admonition shall be further dealt with according to the Scripture and their membership in the church discontinued.

1951, Central District Conference Resolution, Paxton, NE, September 22-25 (CDCY, pp. 16-19)

In the context of concern for the worldwide armament race and the extension of draft legislation, the Conference resolved "that the conference encourage and instruct all its ministers and teachers to lay more emphasis on education for peace, as much needed testimony to a war torn weary world."

1952, Canadian Conference Resolution, Winnipeg, MB, July 5-10 (CCY, pp. 122-125)

From 1952 to 1967 the Canadian Conference almost annually passed resolutions exhorting the churches to further the teaching of the peace position by 1) the organization of peace conferences in each of the Provinces, 2) the instruction of the peace doctrine in all the Bible schools and Christian high schools, 3) the discussion of the peace position at least once a year in the youth groups, 4) the regular proclamation of the peace witness from the pulpits, 5) the observance of a Peace Sunday in November. Because these resolutions become so regular they will not be repeated for each conference (see the following Canadian Conference Yearbooks for these resolutions: 1953, pp. 97-98; 1954, pp. 87-88; 1955, p. 180; 1956, p. 135; 1958, p. 125; 1959, p. 200; 1960, p. 212; 1961, p. 234; 1962, pp. 248-249; 1963, p. 131; 1964, p. 115; 1965, pp. 161-162; 1966, pp. 41-42; 1967, p. 31). Only resolutions which differ from these standard exhortations will be recorded hereafter.

In addition to the above resolutions, the Conference resolved that 1) the churches should invite qualified brethren to conduct teaching/preaching conferences on the peace position, and 2) the churches should introduce all the young people, men and women, to the conference resolution of 1948.

1953, Canadian Conference Resolution, Hepburn, SK, July 4-9 (CCY, pp. 96-98)

The Conference mandated the teaching of the peace position in the churches by 1) the distribution of flyers teaching Biblical nonresistance and the resolutions of the Conference, and 2) the incorporation of the Confession of Faith and the teaching of nonresistance in "the regulations" new church members are expected to observe.

1954, Canadian Conference Resolution, Virgil, ON, July 3-8 (CCY, pp. 85-88)

The Conference authorized the Committee on Nonresistance to negotiate with the government the possibility of recognizing civil defense work as a form of alternative service. Young people were encouraged to participate in civil defense training to be prepared for an emergency, but they were not to participate in any kind of police service.

1954, General Conference Resolution, Hillsboro, KS, October 23-28 (GCY, pp. 114-122)

The noncombatant clause of the 1948 Conference remained a cause of concern to conference leaders. Therefore, a special task force (J.B. Toews and Orlando Harms) was sent to Washington, D.C. immediately following the 1951 General Conference. The men were to explore with the Pentagon the possibilities of noncombatant service within the terms of reference approved by the 1948 and 1951 Conference resolutions. The special concerns of the visit were to determine if noncombatants could serve in the military without taking the military oath and if their role could be defined clearly as the preservation of life rather than the destruction of life. The delegation was informed that l) "the primary purpose of the Medical Corps is not that of saving lives, but removing every obstacle...in the pursuit of the army's assignment to destroy the enemy;" 2) the conscientious objector who serves in the Medical Service "is considered part of the combatant operation" by the military despite any personal convictions or interpretations he may have; 3) "the military oath is an acceptance of combatant status as part of the army" whether or not the CO admits such status.

On the basis of this report from the Board of Reference and Counsel the Conference voted to rescind the 1948 statement on noncombatant service.

The Conference further adopted the following statement as a re-affirmation of the official Confession of Faith with the request that the Board of Reference and Counsel provide additional teaching on the peace position of the Mennonite Brethren Church.

> In stating our convictions we establish no new doctrine, but merely restate the historic faith which our forefathers confirmed

at several occasions. (See Confession of Faith, American Edition, paragraph 66. Also Conference Reports, 1936, pp. 60-63.) Our youth face the issue of participation in war, which obligates us to a clear restatement of our position, thereby reaffirming and strengthening our belief in nonresistance.

The Mennonite Brethren Church believes in non-resistance because:

1. Nonresistance is a biblical principle clearly exemplified by Jesus Christ.

2. The Church as the body of Christ is a fellowship of the redeemed. Therefore, the members are a separated people. John 17:16. They accept Christ as their pattern. I John 2:6. Their lives are controlled by redemptive love. Rom. 5:5.

Since the responsibility of the Church is to present Christ, its Head, and to evangelize the world, participation in any form of war becomes impossible for its members.

3. The practice of the redeemed in Christ demands every phase of their life in all relationships, such as personal, social, national, and international be governed by the supreme law of love, and is not limited to an abstinence from military service. It is a general attitude of the Christian as he seeks the redemption of his fellowmen.

4. Human life is sacred unto God, and a Christian has no right to destroy life.

5. War is evil, brutal and inhuman. It glorifies might, greed and selfishness. The nature of war remains incompatible with the new nature of a regenerated Christian.

6. We declare our sincere loyalty to our government and believe it our duty to respect, obey and pray for our rulers. We would be "subject to the powers that be." In case of a conflict between the demands of the state and the laws of God, the Christian "ought to obey God rather than man." Acts 5:24.

7. We exhort our Christian young men to live consistent with the scriptural and historic testimony of our brotherhood on peace and challenge them to accept the provision of civilian service which our government has made, realizing that this service offers a fuller expression of our scriptural objection to war.

1955, Southern District Conference Resolution, Buhler, KS, October 22-26 (SDCY, p. 73)

The Conference resolved to continue

in loyalty to Christ and love to fellowmen to present a strong, uncompromising witness for peace by a clear personal testimony, by liberal giving, and, if need be, by joyful sacrifice of property, position, conveniences, and suffering for our faith and to continue the conference established custom of using the Sunday nearest Armistice Day as Peace Sunday.

1956, Central District Conference Resolution, Marion, SD, September 29-October 2 (CDCY, pp. 34-35)

The Conference adopted the following resolution on civil defense in response to the extensive preparations for civil defense that were occurring in the United States in the mid-fifties:

The increasing national emphasis upon civil defense in preparation for possible war emergencies calls upon us to carefully evaluate the opportunities and responsibilities of a consistent expression of Scriptural discipleship in our relationships and responsibilities as Christians and citizens.

Civil Defense has been defined by the National Security Resources Board (U.S.A.) thus: 'Civil Defense can be defined as the protection of the home front by civilians acting under civil authority to minimize casualties and war damage and preserve maximum civilian support of the war effort....' Its first objective thus is the preservation of life and property, the second to preserve maximum support of the war effort. As followers of Christ we are committed to all-out support of the first objective but cannot share the second.

In keeping with our historic position of nonparticipation in war because of its conflict with the principles and the example of our Lord and the New Testament teaching, we can therefore lend our support to this effort only to the extent to which it assures us the consistent relation to the first objective--that of preservation.

Our Christian position expressed above places upon us the responsibility as citizens of our country and as Christians and members of our community to cooperation with recognized private and governmental disaster organizations such as Mennonite Disaster Service, Civil Defense, and Red Cross which may be operating in a disaster area where it can be done without violating the accepted Scriptural principles set forth in the nonresistance statement adopted by the Mennonite Brethren Church of North America (Year Book, 1954, pp. 121-122) and to the extent to which we are assured that we are committed to the first objective of the Civil Defense program--the preservation of life and property.

1957, General Conference Resolution, Yarrow, BC, October 20-23 (CGY, pp. 111-113)

The Conference adopted the following statement from the Board of Reference and Counsel in fulfillment of the request of the 1954 Conference for further teaching. The statement was recommended for study and adoption to the various District Conferences.

1. The Church of Jesus Christ is a fellowship of redeemed individuals. The members of the Church are a separated people--called out of darkness into the marvelous light of the children of God. As such we as Mennonite Brethren accept and acknowledge Christ as our Head and the Scriptures as our supreme authority for faith and practice (II Tim. 3:14-17). This relationship to Christ and this acceptance of authority therefore determines our position toward the question of participation in war.

2. Nonresistance is a Biblical principle evincing from the very tenor of the New Testament teachings regarding the practical Christian life and is, of course, clearly exemplified by Jesus Christ. To 'those who by reason of use have their senses exercised to discern both good and evil' (Heb. 5:14) the doctrine of nonresistance is almost self-evident. But Biblical nonresistance is not pacifism; it arises from an entirely different motive and the two are propagated by two entirely different groups of people. Scripturally speaking, it arises from the fact of the believer's:

1) *new nature* miraculously imparted when he was born again (Eph. 4:22-24, 31-32; Col.: 3.8-10);

2) *new relationship* to Jesus Christ which in turn affects his total relationship to God, to man and the the world through the acceptance of Christ as Saviour and Lord (Rom. 6:4; I Cor 12:13; II Cor: 5.17; Eph.: 5.1);

3) *new walk* prescribed in Scriptures which leaves no room for activities and attitudes naturally expected of soldiers (Rom. 8:1, 4; Eph. 4:1; 5:10, 15; Col. 2:6);

4) *new citizenship and loyalty* (Eph. 2:19; Phil. 3:20, R.V.); there is no New Testament call upon the Christian to fight 'a defensive war,' or 'war to end war,' or 'to save the world for democracy,' or even to establish a state of righteousness. This leads us to the next logical assertion, i.e., that the doctrine of nonresistance arises from the fact of the believer's

5) *new warfare* (John 18:36; II Cor. 10:3-6). The spiritual warfare as described in these references is in essence diametrically opposed to the methods, instruments and objectives of physical warfare;

6) *new mission.* The Christian's first and foremost duty is to serve and glorify God. This duty is not partial, optional or secondary. The promotion of the work of Christ is every Christian's primary mission. The nature of this mission is such that active participation in war, the bearing of arms for destruction of human life, by a born again believer constitutes a serious violation of the fixed principle laid down by Christ and Paul as expressed in Luke 9:62 and II Tim. 2:4 respectively. A Christian is not at liberty to take leave from this commission that for a season 'he may please him who hath chosen him to be a soldier.'

7) *new life principle—love.* According to Christ, love is the chief mark of discipleship as well as the chief New Testament commandment (John 13:34-34, 15:10, 12, 17-19). Can a man destroy a fellow man while he loves him? The Apostle John holds that it is impossible. Speaking of one who 'shutteth up his bowels of compassion from his brother,' he asks, 'how dwelleth the love of God in him?' (I John 3.17). We do not, even as the State does not, believe in 'mercy killing;' much less do we believe it possible to kill while we love. Therefore, our path is clear; we dare not be motivated or determined in our actions and relationships by anything but love 'shed abroad into our

hearts' (Rom. 5:5), and 'faith that worketh by love' (Gal. 5:6). Hence, we cannot take human life even in self-defense.

3. Practically speaking, the living out of the principle of Biblical nonresistance is but daring to apply to our daily activities and relationships what Jesus Christ, the Captain of our Salvation, has taught and exemplified and is but one phase of virile discipleship. The principle of nonresistance, therefore, is not limited to war. We believe and teach that it applies to every phase of our life, to all relationships, personal, social, economic, political, national and international. The whole of the Christian personality must be integrated around the Person of Jesus Christ as He has revealed Himself in redemptive love according to the Scriptures (Luke 6:29-37; Rom. 12:1, 2; I Thess. 5:23).

4. War is evil, brutal, and inhuman. The fact that Jesus said 'there shall be wars and rumors of wars' cannot justly be construed to be His stamp of approval upon war. As one militarist has said, 'War is the sink of all evil.' It glorifies might, greed, lust and selfishness. The nature of war has ever been, is now, and will remain incompatible with the new nature, relationship, walk, citizenship, loyalty, warfare, mission and principle of life of the regenerated Christian (James 4:1-5). Paul admonishes the Ephesians to 'have no fellowship with the unfruitful works of darkness, but rather reprove them' (5:11). Though the context does not here directly deal with the activities and consequences of war, what words could better describe them?

5. The New Testament allows the Christian only one view of man: we look upon every person as a soul 'for whom Christ died' (I Cor. 8:11), needing to be, and potentially capable of being saved. How dare we cut short his days and thereby his chances to accept the grace of God?

6. We declare our unequivocal loyalty to our government and gladly own our duty to respect, obey and pray for and be 'subject to the powers that be.' Our services and properties are at the disposal of our government for the alleviation of need and the saving of lives. We are willing to sacrifice for our country and the welfare of others. In the case of conflict between the demands of the State and the laws of God, however, the Christian 'ought to obey God rather than man.' Acts 5.29.

7. We, therefore, exhort our Christian young men to live consistent with the Scriptural teaching and historic testimony of our Brotherhood and challenge them to accept the provision of civilian service which our government has made, realizing that this provision offers an acceptable expression of our Scriptural objection to war (I Cor. 15:58) but under no circumstance to accept responsibilities that demand the destruction of human life. These things we believe and teach. These are our convictions. In the words of the great Martin Luther,

> Here we stand;
> We can do no other
> So help us God.

In the meantime we are eagerly looking for and hastening unto the day of our Lord's return when Christ, the Captain of our Salvation, will rapture the Church, and then together with His saints come back to earth as the Prince of Peace to establish His Kingdom of Righteousness and men shall learn war no more. 'And they shall not hurt nor destroy...for the earth shall be full of the knowledge of the Lord as the waters cover the sea' (Isa. 11:9).

1958, Canadian Conference Resolution, North Kildonan, MB, July 5-9 (CCY, pp. 124-125)

The Conference resolved that the book "True Nonresistance through Christ" by John A. Toews, which had been written and published by Conference mandate in 1955, should be distributed to all churches in the ratio of 10 copies per 100 members.

1958, Southern District Conference Resolution, Enid, OK, October 18-22 (SDCY, pp. 40-43)

The Conference adopted the 1957 General Conference statement on nonresistance with minor editorial changes and the addition of a final paragraph. The concluding paragraph reads as follows:

> Finally, we are called upon as believers to a life of total discipleship. Should another war break upon us, the sharp distinctions we make in classifying our young men might well fall away. In view of modern warfare we will be forced to take one position or the other: either we will be total Christians in the Kingdom of

Christ or we will be in the kingdom of the world. The specific choice before us in the future will not be between taking a I-A or a I-A-O position, but between taking our position wholly with Christ and the Church or with the kingdom of evil and destruction. He who takes his position with Christ will be brought directly to the Cross and may be asked to give his life. This will be the supreme choice we will be challenged to make. It is not a choice of classification, first of all, but a choice of supreme and uncompromising loyalty to Christ.

1960, Canadian Conference Resolution, Virgil, ON, July 2-6 (CCY, pp. 212-213)

The conference agreed that the peace position be taught systematically in the churches and schools of the Conference "so that we might not only refuse to take part in war, but also in police and jury service and similar services."

This resolution was repeated again in 1961 (see CCY, p. 234) and 1962 (see CCY, pp. 248-249).

1968, Canadian Conference Resolution, Clearbrook, BC, July 6-8 (CCY, pp. 40-68, 101-107)

The 1968 Canadian Conference was a "Faith and Life" Study Conference. Two issues were studied, the peace witness and situation ethics. The pattern of the Conference was to hear a series of papers on the issue, discuss the issue in small groups, adopt "a declaration of the Conference" statement as the position of the Conference on the issue. The peace witness papers were presented by H.R. Baerg, John A. Toews, and John Redekop. The "Declaration of the Conference," which went through three public revisions before adoption, reads as follows:

The Needs Calling for a Re-Examination of our Peace Witness

1. The world with its moral, spiritual and political confusion, gravitating toward self annihilation in hopeless despair, is seeking a solution and way of peace for itself without apparent success.
2. Since the church including evangelicals has been involved in war, and often in the history of the world have been active

advocates in war, and often in the history of the world have been active advocates of violence, the world is confused as to the role of the church in its relationship to peace: and therefore questions the primacy and relevancy of the Gospel of Christ.

3. The church including the Mennonite Brethren is facing questions of immediate and long range importance relating to current problems of government, industry, racism, war, etc. The church needs to know how it speaks to these issues.

4. Pragmatic pacifism is on the increase and its advocates look to the evangelicals of the peace church for cooperation and support, while these evangelicals flounder, not knowing if they can join hands with humanistic pacifists to proclaim Christian peace.

5. There is a questioning among members of our Conference as to the validity and scope of our peace position, which calls for a re-assessment and re-formulation of our statements on peace.

6. The evangelical church with its message of forgiveness of sins, life and peace in the person of Jesus Christ, needs to discover channels of communication whereby it makes this message of redemption and peace known to all strata of society in all the world.

7. While we express concern about national and international conflicts, often so little of the true spirit of Christ finds expression in interpersonal relationships, in community, home, church, and economic affairs.

8. Since MCC has acted as spokesman for Mennonite Churches in speaking to government on issues relating to our peace position and other political issues, it is felt that a re-examination of MCC's responsibilities in this regard is needed.

The Basis of our Peace Witness

1. We accept God's total progressive revelation as found in the Old and New Testament and in Christ, his exemplary life, teaching and redemptive death as a basis for our peace position. Heb. 1:1-2.

2. Having received Jesus Christ personally by invitation and having experienced a work of regeneration in our hearts by the Holy Spirit, we consider ourselves nonresistant and responsible for a peace witness. This distinguishes us from the philosophical and political pacifists, who from a humanistic point of view

seek to advocate peace. Titus 3:3-7; I Cor. 6:6-11; II Cor. 5:17; I Peter 2:1, 2, 19-24.

3. The Spirit filled life expresses itself in love, joy, peace, long-suffering, gentleness, goodness, faith, meekness and temperance, as stated in Galatians 5:22-23 and I Corinthians 13. Peace is not superior nor inferior to other virtues mentioned in Scripture but in conjunction with other virtues governs all our interpersonal relationships.

4. Governments are ordained by God for the purpose of providing order, protection, and judgment. God has placed responsibilities and powers into the hands of government which are not the direct responsibilities of the church. It is therefore the believers' responsibility to subject himself to government, to pay taxes, to pray for the powers that be, and for the sake of conscience live an exemplary Christian life. When government's orders to its subjects are contrary to God's commands, then the believer is responsible to obey God rather than man. Romans 13:1-7; Acts 5:29; I Timothy 2:1-6; I Peter 2:13-15.

5. With the knowledge of God's estimate of human life and that man has an eternal immortal soul, we in our peace witness desire to spare man's life and through our witness, make him receptive, so that we can proclaim to him the Gospel of Christ with invitation to receive him as Lord and Saviour. I Timothy 2:1-5.

6. The church speaks authoritatively in application of our peace witness only when Scripture clearly speaks to the issue; when Scripture is silent, the church seeks to establish a brotherhood consensus to unite members in their interpretation but leaves room for personal interpretation and application to the individual.

Declarations Re Our Peace Witness

1. Current opportunities

That we, who carry the conviction for peace witness be alert to current developments within our church and our world society in which we can offer a positive Christian peace witness.

2. Obedience to Government

That we support the government in its efforts to maintain law, order and justice. When the demands of the government are contrary to Scripture, the church or individual should be prepared to obey God rather than man, regardless of the consequences. The spirit of Scripture does not allow any agitation for or inciting to rebellion; and any civil disobedience is to be justified only by response to biblical teaching.

3. Military Service

That we, in commitment to Christ and the Scripture, in a spirit of gratitude offer to our country constructive, alternative service in time of peace or war, since we cannot participate in military service intended to destroy life.

4. Church Speaking to Government

That we as a church, through the officially chosen executive personnel, continue to communicate to government our position on moral issues including our peace witness. However, this does not absolve the individual citizen from expressing his Christian convictions to government.

5. Demonstrations

That we, as a church, believe that the spirit of Scripture does not encourage participation in protest marches or demonstrations. We need to be considerate, however, when a member of the church, after prayerful evaluation of the purpose and the associations of the demonstration arrives at the personal conviction that he should participate.

6. Race Relations

That we, with respect to racial relations, declare that all races are equal before God and that we need to give evidence of this conviction by identifying ourselves with them through love and acceptance in personal and group relationships. Where race conflicts could develop or already exist we should be willing to become involved in practical ministries which can help toward reconciliation.

7. Labour Relations

That we, in view of our peace witness, stand for peaceful negotiations between labour and management in the settlement of disputes. By this we understand that when we find ourselves in the midst of dispute we do not allow ourselves to become involved in any violence or the threat of violence; that we, in as far as opportunities necessitate suffer loss rather than compromise

Christian principles; that we, whether employer or employee, be governed by the Spirit of Christ in an attempt to give expression to the Christian virtues listed in Galatians 5:22-23.

8. Inter-Church Peace Witnessing

That we, in recognizing that our peace witness cannot be separated from our mission to evangelize, periodically assess our relationship with other denominations to whom we relate in our peace position: and that we actively seek the participation of and with evangelical churches who share our concerns on peace issues.

9. Teaching

That we commit ourselves to a teaching ministry in our homes, churches and mission fields which includes instruction on our peace position: and that we emphasize that the peace position be related to practical issues in every day life.

1969, Canadian Conference Resolution, Winnipeg, MB, July 5-8 (CCY, pp. 46-48)

The 1969 Conference reaffirmed a slightly edited version of the 1968 "Declaration" on the recommendation of the Board of Spiritual and Social Concerns (the new name for the Board of Reference and Counsel).

1969, General Conference Resolutions, Vancouver, BC, August 23-26 (GCY, pp. 44, 85, 113-114)

The 1969 Conference addressed the peace question in two different ways.

First of all, the Board of Reference and Counsel presented a revised draft of the Confession of Faith as authorized by the 1966 Conference. The proposed article on "love and nonresistance" (Article XV) reads as follows:

We believe that Christians should live by the law of love and practice forgiveness of enemies as taught and exemplified by the Lord Jesus. The church, as the body of Christ, is a fellowship of redeemed, separated people, controlled by redemptive love. Her responsibility to present Christ, the Prince of peace, to the world as the answer for human enmity and violence is incompatible with retaliation, revenge and warfare. The evil, brutal and inhuman nature of war stands in contradiction to the new nature of the regenerated Christian. The Christian seeks to practice Christ's law of love in all relationships (personal, social, national and international), at all times (war and peace), and in all situations (including those involving personal injustice, social upheaval and international tensions). Instead of participating in the military we accept an alternative area of service which will serve to reduce strive, alleviate suffering and bear witness to the love of Christ. Ex. 20:1-17; Matt. 5:17-28, 38-45; Rom. 10:4; 12:19-21; 13:8-10; Col. 2:16-23; 1 Pet. 2:19-23.

The revised draft was presented as a working draft for the consideration of the churches.

Secondly, the Conference was asked to support a resolution presented by several young people to denounce "the participation of all governments in the Vietnam war," to "support political candidates who hold responsibly to the peace position regarding Vietnam," to "oppose the US selective service system and other such necessities of war wherever they exist," and to "support draft resisters and resistance movements."

The Conference responded to this request in two different ways. 1) The Reference and Counsel presented the following statements:

As a Conference we wish to acknowledge the legitimate concerns of those among us who are sensitive to the absence of a statement at this convention regarding our position on war and associated evils. We wish to call to the delegates' attention a Conference resolution passed at the 1954 Convention, a portion of which reads as follows: "The Mennonite Brethren Church believes in nonresistance because...nonresistance is a biblical principle clearly exemplified by Jesus Christ...participation in any form of war becomes impossible...War is evil, brutal and inhuman. It glorifies might, greed and selfishness. The nature of war remains incompatible with the new nature of a redeemed Christian.'

We are persuaded, however, that a more recent statement on the above named subject is needed. We recommend that a study in depth be carried on during the next triennium on the subject of involvement in war, and that a resolution be presented at the 1972 Convention.

The Reference and Counsel did not feel it could say more at the Conference because the proposed resolution had not come through proper conference channels, raised issues that required a study conference process, and addressed specifically United States issues that some Canadian delegates did not feel should be considered at a conference held in Canada.

The Conference leadership was restless about this initial response, however. Therefore, later in the Convention the Board of Reference and Counsel proposed the following resolution:

> The fifty-first General Conference of Mennonite Brethren Churches in session at Vancouver, B.C., August 23-26, 1969, re-affirms its historic position on peace and nonresistance and against war in keeping with its Confession of Faith and its understanding of Scriptural teaching.
>
> We believe that the Christian's new life in Christ makes it inconsistent for him to participate in war or the destruction of life. The believer accepts Christ as his pattern (I John 2:6; I Peter 2:21) and his life is to be controlled by redemptive love (Rom. 5:5; Matt. 5:44).
>
> We believe that war and violence are incompatible with the nature and calling of the Church. The Church is called to a ministry of reconciliation and restoration of man's broken relationships to God and his fellowmen. War disrupts these relationships and destroys moral and spiritual values by its greed, selfishness and cruelty. In the present world of unrest we recognize our Christian responsibility personally to live consistently with the principles of love and peace, as well as to promote peace and good will in inter-personal, inter-group, and inter-national relations. The same principles shall apply in racial and industrial conflicts.
>
> We believe that Christians must be 'subject to the powers that be' (Rom. 13:1). However, this subjection is limited by the believer's primary loyalty to Christ, his Savior and Lord. In any conflict between the demands of the state and the commands of Christ, the Christian 'ought to obey God rather than man' (Acts 5:29).

We believe that the Church has a prophetic role in relation to the state. Whenever the government fails in its divinely ordained function of administering justice and promoting peace, it is the Christian's responsibility to express his concern, and to witness against the abuses of power and the miscarriage of justice.

We believe that as Christians we should serve our government only in such ways as are in keeping with our faith and redemptive mission. We appeal, therefore, to all our members to accept some form of civilian service when they are called to serve their country.

As a Brotherhood we pledge ourselves to seek prayerfully a fuller understanding and a more adequate expression of our Christian responsibility in a world of unrest.

The resolution was referred to Reference and Counsel for the preparation of "a fuller statement" to be published in the Conference periodicals as a Board of Reference and Counsel statement.

1969, Pacific District Conference Resolution, Sacramento, CA, November 7-9 (PDCY, pp. 4-6, 31)

A group of young people submitted a question to the Conference asking the Conference to reaffirm the historic peace position of the Mennonite Brethren Confession of Faith, and to recognize non-cooperation with the Selective Service as a valid form of conscientious objection.

The Conference responded with the following resolution:

We reaffirm the Mennonite Brethren position on nonresistance as presented to the 1954 General Conference (see 1954 General Conference Yearbook or Appendix to the submitted question). We likewise reaffirm that this position on nonresistance is founded on a biblical basis and not on mere humanistic concern. We concur with the expressed concern of our young people regarding the need for greater emphasis on the biblical teaching on nonresistance.

The historic position of the Mennonite Brethren in relation to civil government is in agreement with biblical teaching as found in Romans 13:1-7. Our Christian commitment respects law and order and we pray for those who are in authority. In circumstances where the demands of civil government are in conflict with our commitment to Christ and biblical teachings, we accept the possible consequences even to the extent of suffering and death. We believe that our voice against unrighteousness in civil government is not to be heard in political pronouncements but through the channel of responsible Christian citizenship as individuals.

Selective service is a recruiting agency; it is not necessarily a vehicle of destruction. For those who desire, it can become an agency for positive Christian service and the peace witness by accepting alternative service.

We are grateful to our government for the provision which it makes for the possibility of alternative civilian service. In light of the existing positive service opportunities authorized through Selective Service, we as a Conference cannot support non-cooperation with Selective Service as a valid peace witness. We urge our young people to accept constructive alternative service as provided by our government. However, we believe that our churches should extend a spiritual ministry to those who because of personal conviction take the position of non-cooperation with Selective Service.

Our witness as a church in a day of world conflict, social revolution and spiritual tensions requires an ever increasing degree of brotherly love and sympathetic understanding. In patience and lowliness of mind we must esteem others better than ourselves. In dedication to Christ, let us work in the unity of the Spirit to do God's will in a world of great spiritual need.

1969, Southern District Conference Resolution, Buhler, KS, November 14-16 (SDCY, pp. 9-11, 70-71)

The Committee of Reference and Counsel presented a statement on the "Christian Responsibility in a Time of Civil Unrest." The part which addressed the peace witness reads as follows:

The Committee of Reference and Counsel believes that a word should be spoken at this convention regarding our attitude toward the present world situation. God has not left us without direction concerning the Christian's relationship to his government and to the society in which he lives. Two basic scriptural passages are Romans 12:17-13:7 and I Peter 2:9-25. From these pertinent passages we call your attention to the following excerpts taken from the *Living Letters* paraphrase: 'Never pay back evil for evil...Be at peace with everyone just as much as you possibly can...Don't let evil get the upper hand but conquer evil by doing good. Obey the government, for God is the One who has put it there. There is no government anywhere that God has not placed into power. So those who refuse to obey the laws of the land are refusing to obey God, and punishment will follow...You must obey the laws for two reasons: to keep from being punished and because you know you should...Obey those over you and give honor and respect to all those to whom it is due...For the Lord's sake, obey every law of your government...You are free from the law, but that does not mean you are free to do wrong. Live as those who are free to do only God's will at all times. Show respect for everyone. Love Christians everywhere. Fear God and honor the government.' When the demands of government and God conflict, then the Scripture teaches that the Christian's highest allegiance must be to God. The question raised in Acts 4:19 'You decide whether God wants us to obey you instead of Him' is answered in Acts 5:29: 'We must obey God rather than men.' *Living New Testament*

In view of the Scriptural instruction and the temper of our times, we express thanks to God for the attempts of our government and the President of the United States to achieve peace, and we encourage continued efforts to this end, and assure the President of our continued prayers. Furthermore, we express our appreciation to the Selective Service for its considerate recognition of the position of the historic peace churches and to the provision for alternative opportunities for expression of our faith in positive and constructive ways throughout the world.

We express our continued interest in and support of causes of peace and reconciliation in keeping with the principles of Biblical nonresistance. We encourage extreme caution and discernment regarding identification with resistance movements, some of whose activities encourage the overthrow of the government.

1971, United States Conference Resolution, Denver, CO, August 13-15 (USCY, p. 35)

The Conference re-affirmed the historic peace position of the Mennonite Brethren Church while refusing to support non-cooperation with the Selective Service, as requested by some young people in 1969.

> The historic position of the Mennonite Brethren regarding a Christian's relationship to civil government is based on such Scriptures as Romans 13:1-7, I Timothy 2:1-4, and Acts 5:29. As those who hold citizenship in two worlds Christians must respect, obey and pray for those in authority. On the other hand, where demands of civil government conflict with biblical teaching, Christians are to obey Christ rather than man and be willing to accept the consequences of suffering or even death. Strong protest against unrighteousness in civil government can be made through individual responsible Christian citizenship.
>
> The concerns of our brotherhood in problems of war, peace and nonresistance are as old as our history. More recent references are made in minutes of the General Conference sessions of 1954 and 1969.
>
> In a time when such concern is popular among many, we must clarify our position as being founded not only on humanistic concern, but on biblical teaching. We are glad for the interest of many of our young people for greater emphasis on the biblical teaching of nonresistance.
>
> We are grateful to God that our government recognizes our peace position and allows alternatives to military service; alternatives which can be positive and constructive expressions of our faith and love. We urge our young people to accept the alternatives provided, especially those of our Christian Service Program.
>
> While Selective Service was established basically as a means for the recruitment of men for the armed forces; for those who choose it may become an agency for recruitment for Christian

service and a peace witness. In light of the Scriptures and offered alternatives, we believe we should not support non-cooperation with Selective Service. On the other hand, a spiritual ministry should be extended to those who because of personal conviction take a position of non-cooperation.

Our constant aim must be to live in accordance with the wishes of God,'...who desires all men to be saved and come to the knowledge of the truth' (I Timothy 2:4).

1972, General Conference Resolution, Reedley, CA, November 11-14 (GCY, p. 22)

The sixth edition of the revised Confession of Faith was presented. Article XV on "Love and Nonresistance" was presented in its 1969 form with only slight editorial changes. This revised Confession was referred to the Canadian and United States Conferences for study and discussion. It was agreed that the 1975 General Conference would consider only those questions raised by the national conferences before formally adopting the Confession of Faith.

1975, General Conference Resolution, Winnipeg, MB, August 9-12 (GCY, pp. 15-17)

The seventh revised draft of the Confession of Faith was adopted.

Only two amendments to the proposed draft were approved, one concerning Article XV. It was agreed to amend the last sentence to read, "We believe that it is not God's will that Christians take up arms in military service but that, where possible they perform alternative service to reduce strife, alleviate suffering and bear witness to the love of Christ."

The official Mennonite Brethren Confession of Faith on "Love and Nonresistance" adopted in 1975 now reads as follows:

We believe that Christians should live by the law of love and practice the forgiveness of enemies as taught and exemplified by the Lord Jesus. The church, as the body of Christ, is a fellowship of redeemed, separated people, controlled by redemptive love. Its evangelistic responsibility is to present Christ, the Prince of Peace, as the answer to human need, enmity and violence. The evil, brutal and inhuman nature of war stands in contradiction to the new nature of the Christian. The Christian seeks to practice Christ's law of love in all relationships, and in all situations, including those involving personal injustice, social upheaval and international tensions. We believe it is not God's will that Christians take up arms in military service but that, where possible they perform alternative service to reduce strife, alleviate suffering and bear witness to the love of Christ. Ex. 20:1-7; Matt. 5:17-28, 38-45; Rom. 12:19-21; 13:8-10; I Pet. 2:19-23.

The Board of Reference and Counsel at this Conference also issued a statement authored by J.A. Toews, "Our Ministry of Reconciliation in a Broken World," as its official response to the motion of the 1969 General Conference requesting the publication of a "fuller statement" on the peace position. The published pamphlet was given to each delegate at the Conference and sent to all pastors and churches as a Board of Reference and Counsel statement. (The pamphlet is not reprinted here because of its length and because it is available from Kindred Press.)

1979, Pacific District Conference Resolution, Bakersfield, CA, November 8-10 (PDCY, pp. 44-47)

The Board of Reference and Counsel responded to some church members who felt the peace position was unpopular and thus an embarrassment to the Mennonite Brethren Church and to some others who felt the peace position was an optional distinctive of earlier Anabaptism that was not central to the gospel.

The Board reaffirmed the peace witness of the Mennonite Brethren Church with the following statement:

> The *Confession of Faith* states, 'We believe that Christians should live by the law of love...The Christian seeks to practice Christ's law of love in all relationships, and in all situations ...'
>
> Consequently, we affirm:
>
> (1) the need to broaden our understanding of this article of faith as being descriptive of our total way of life; and to seek applications of this teaching in our homes, schools, and churches, in labor relations, race relations, domestic (family)

relations, professional relations, and state relations, etc., (as well as in military situations).

(2) the need for our pastors and teachers to actively preach and teach the importance of this teaching of Jesus for our contemporary life.

(3) the need for more church dialogue and discussion in convenient forums such as new members' classes, Christian Education classes, Bible studies, peace seminars, and via literature, films, drama, etc.

(4) the need for our College and Seminary and other Conference agencies to strengthen the Biblical teaching on the basis of this article of the *Confession*.

(5) the need for our Pacific District Board of Reference and Counsel to actively counsel those in pastoral leadership to personally study the biblical basis for this article of the *Confession* in order to ensure growth beyond a position of neutrality.

(6) the need to recommit ourselves as a brotherhood (covenant community) to the validity and viability of our *Confession of Faith*.

(7) the need to practice in our local churches what we confess and preach relative to love and peacemaking. For those who have chosen, or choose, some form of military service we urge that a spirit of love and reconciliation prevail, not as an accommodation of our position but as an expression of it.

The biblically based doctrine of Jesus' limitless love is not an option, nor a denominational hobby horse. It is a vital and intrinsic part of God's Word for our world. 'As the Father has loved me, so have I loved you: *continue ye in my love'* (Jn. 15:9).

1980, United States Conference Resolution, Minneapolis, MN, August 14-17 (USCY, pp. 9-12)

The Board of Reference and Counsel, following a Peace Study Conference in Hillsboro, Kansas, March 19-20, 1980, presented a comprehensive seven point resolution that was designed to address a wide range of war-peace issues current in the United States churches at the time. The resolution read as follows:

(1) We recommend that all members practice Christian love based on the life and teachings of Jesus by constantly seeking,

through God's grace, to demonstrate a nonretaliatory lifestyle and to be peacemakers and reconcilers.

(2) We recommend that all members comply with the government's request to register. This is compatible with our understanding of the Scriptures as expressed in Article XIV of our Confession of Faith.

(3) We recommend that those drafted accept alternative service assignments in lieu of military service in keeping with our understanding of God's Word as expressed in Article XV. The alternative service arrangements must require sacrifical service assignments related to significant human need, be under the guidance of pastoral care and be supported at a cost to the church.

(4) We recognize those who, for Christian conscience' sake, choose to enter noncombatant service. We express reservation about noncombatant service because it requires taking the military oath. (See M.B. General Conference Minutes, 1954, pp. 115-122.)

(5) We recognize those who, for Christian conscience' sake, choose not to cooperate by not responding to the military draft. We express reservation about this position because of aspects relating to civil disobedience. (See Article XIV in our Confession of Faith.)

(6) We cannot endorse the principle of civil disobedience when incompatible with the Word of God as expressed in Article XIV of our Confession of Faith.

(7) We recommend that all members consider all people-destroying attitudes and actions, whether individual or corporate (such as military combat), as incompatible with God's will for His children as expressed in Article XV of our Confession of Faith.

The resolution provoked intense controversy and dissent because of the specificity of its statements. In the end a less specific resolution was overwhelmingly approved by the Conference.

1. We affirm our M.B. Confession of Faith and historic peace position.

2. We recognize that some members of our churches and some

other churches do not fully agree with our confessional understanding of the Scriptures, and we commit ourselves to loving and accepting relationships with such members and churches.

3. We emphasize the need for more systematic Bible teaching in our churches regarding peace making.

1981, General Conference Resolution, St. Catharines, ON, August 7-11 (GCY, pp. 50-51)

The Conference, reflecting growing concern about some churches and some pastors who either did not accept or even opposed the historic peace stance of the Mennonite Brethren Church, adopted the following resolution:

The Mennonite Brethren Confession of Faith states:

'We believe that Christians should live by the law of love and practice the forgiveness of enemies as taught and exemplified by the Lord Jesus. The church, the body of Christ, is a fellowship of redeemed, separated people, controlled by redemptive love. Its evangelistic responsibility is to present Christ, the Prince of Peace, as the answer to human need, enmity and violence. The evil brutal inhuman nature of war stands in contradiction to the new nature of the Christian. The Christian seeks to practice Christ's law of love in all relationships, and in all situations, including those involving personal injustice, social upheaval and international tensions. We believe that it is not God's will that Christians take up arms in military service but that, where possible, they perform alternative service to reduce strife, alleviate suffering and bear witness to the love of Christ' (p. 21).

We are concerned that a goodly number of our church members (including some pastors) view our position on 'love and nonresistance' as an optional doctrine. In some churches this doctrine is not taught; in some it is even opposed; and in some instances young men are even encouraged to take up arms in military service. This we consider to be a serious violation of our peace position and of the teachings of Jesus, as we have understood these in our history.

In the preface to our Confession of Faith it is stated that confessions of faith are not to be given equal status with the Bible. That is in keeping with our position that the Bible is our highest authority and that our understanding of it is never perfect, and that we must, therefore, always be open to new light.

However, when we accepted the present Confession of Faith in 1975 that represented our church's understanding of the main doctrines of the Scripture, and such a Confession can be changed or modified only when our conference comes to a new understanding of some article in our confession through the study of the Scriptures.

We recognize that not all believers share our understanding of this biblical teaching, but we would strongly urge that when churches call pastors they make sure that they adhere to all the articles in our Confession of Faith. Those churches and boards in our provinces and districts that process the ordination of brothers for the pastoral ministry should insure that the person to be ordained shares our conference's position on 'love and nonresistance.' Also, pastors are encourage to make sure that this doctrine is taught.

1982, Pacific District Conference Resolution, Visalia, CA, November 11-13 (PDCY, pp. 48-50)

The Board of Reference and Counsel recommended the following "Statement on Nuclear Disarmament."

In 1982 we have witnessed a fast growing awareness and concern in the United States over the issue of nuclear warfare. Hardly a day goes by without some newspaper or magazine questioning the wisdom and morality of a further escalation of the nuclear arms race. At the same time a diversified movement has grown up both inside and outside the church at large in support of a nuclear weapons freeze as a first step towards disarmament. Such notable evangelical spokesmen as Billy Graham, Ted Engstrom (World Vision), Vernon Grounds (President Emeritus, Conservative Baptist Theological Seminary), and David McKenna (President, Asbury Theological Seminary), among others, have spoken in favor of such a course of action.

The question of how Mennonite Brethren Churches should be involved in this effort has received serious attention by your Board of Reference and Counsel this year along with many other issues and needs...

In order to properly fulfill our role of watching over the spiritual health and concerns of our churches and to provide direction in this specific area we have felt it important to remind ourselves of the words of our Mennonite Brethren Confession, which states, 'our evangelistic responsibility is to present Christ, the Prince of Peace, as the answer to human need, enmity and violence.'

On the basis of this understanding of our Christian responsibility to promote the pursuit of peace we of the Board of Reference and Counsel share this plea with you today and with all Christians everywhere. We join with many other Christians in our nation and around the world in expressing our objection to the further development of nuclear weaponry. The investment of human, natural and economic resources in the further proliferation of nuclear weapons reduces the capacity of all governments to contribute to the wellbeing of their citizens and to all people of the world. The existence of these powerful weapons of destruction threatens the death and diminished capacities of entire populations for generations to come. The existence and proliferation of nuclear weapons is, therefore, a sin against God and creation. In proclaiming the whole Gospel of God in Jesus Christ, we are compelled to address this evil for which we as citizens of earthly kingdoms share responsibility.

At the same time we as Christians should repent of any implicit or explicit approval we may have given to the nation that the threatened use of nuclear weapons is justified and moral. In the light of God's Word it is neither.

We plead, therefore, for an immediate world-wide freeze on the testing, production, and deployment of nuclear weapons and we further plead for a staged, mutual and verifiable reduction of existing nuclear arsenals leading to the eventual abolition of all nuclear weapons.

In conclusion, the Bible calls us to pray 'for kings and all who are in authority in order that we may lead a quiet life in all godlines and dignity' (I Timothy 2:1-2). Let us pray in this manner and then diligently pursue the things that make for peace.

The resolution was so controversial that it was tabled for further study.

1984, Canadian Conference Resolutions, Clearbrook, BC, July 6-9 (CCY, pp. 103-105)

The Conference approved two peace resolutions, one on participation in peace marches and a second on the nuclear threat, in response to questions from churches and individuals.

The peace march resolution asserts that

The basis of our peace witness is found in the exemplary life, teaching and death of Jesus Christ. It is an expression of the Spirit-filled life. Therefore, any public or private expression of this witness needs to be in harmony with the above.

The first statement concerning peace marches was made by the conference in Clearbrook in 1968. It concluded as follows: '...we as a church have no scriptural mandate to participate in protest marches or demonstrations because: a) demonstrations are usually not motivated by Biblical principles, b) the believer's responsibility toward the government is to be a law-abiding citizen and not a revolutionary or agitator to incite people.

We need to be considerate, however, when a member of a church, after careful evaluation of the purposes and associations of the march arrives at the personal conviction that he should participate' (Canadian Conference Yearbook, 1968, pp. 67-68).

A. We believe peace marches have certain limitations such as:

1. Our witness for peace on the basis of our relationship to our Lord, the Prince of Peace, can be lost or diluted as we march with those who seek peace for humanistic, humanitarian or political reasons.

2. The aggressive, military spirit of some peace marches contradicts the spirit of meekness and willingness to suffer for Christ that should mark the Christian's peace witness.

3. Participation in a peace march can easily be seen as the total responsibility to witness for peace. It is probably easier to march for peace than to live by the principles that encourage peace in everday lives.

B. On the other hand, we believe peace walks (we prefer this term to 'peace marches' because of militant overtones) have value for the following reasons:

1. They effectively raise the consciousness of the issue of war, peace and destruction because they offer a great deal of visibility.

2. They are a way of taking our faith into the streets and offer opportunity to witness to spectators and those with whom we walk.

3. They offer the opportunity of individualized banners that more clearly project our basis for a peace witness and thus serve as an educational tool.

4. They could serve as a first step of a commitment to witness for peace and lead to a life that expresses the principles of discipleship daily.

In view of the above we recommend that: Participation in peace walks that do not violate or compromise our peace position, but rather enhance it, can be recognized as a positive witness. Individuals or groups are advised, however, to prayerfully seek guidance and counsel from the Word and from the local community of believers before participating.

The "nuclear threat" resolution reads as follows:

We live in a time when people's hearts tremble and fear, fear that we are reaching the end of the road. With the psalmist we are compelled to pray, 'Teach us to number our days that we may apply our hearts to wisdom.'

We confess:

that we have neglected to teach and to practice the whole message of peace that Jesus brought.

that at times we have neglected to intercede for those in authority and have been unduly critical.

that we take seriously the admonition to pray for political leaders who are responsible for major decisions related to the nuclear threat (I Tim. 2:1-3).

that we take seriously the admonition to pray for our enemies (Luke 6:27; Rom. 12:20).

that we take seriously the great commission, proclaiming the whole gospel of Jesus Christ so that all people will be saved (Matt. 28:19-20).

that we take seriously our responsibility to work for peace and reconciliation wherever there is a potential for conflict (Matt. 5:9).

that we will seriously search for ways to speak responsibly to political leaders regarding our concern for the safety of the people of this global village.

that we will call on our leaders and our teachers to present clear teaching on issues pertaining to reconciliation and peace (2 Tim. 3:16).

that we will call on our people to put their confidence in God who continues to exercise His sovereign power and will to overrule in world affairs (Psalm 2:1-6).

Sources of the Appendix

The appendix is based on the following Mennonite Brethren Conference Yearbooks:

General Conference, 1878-1984
Central District Conference, 1910-1985
Southern District Conference, 1910-1984
Northern/Canadian Conference, 1910-1985
Pacific District Conference, 1912-1984
United States Conference, 1957-1984